DEATH
Philosophical Soundings

DEATH
Philosophical Soundings

Herbert Fingarette

OPEN COURT

Chicago and La Salle, Illinois

The following publishers have given permission to use extended quotations from copyrighted works. From *The Stranger* by Albert Camus, trans. Stuart Gilbert. Copyright 1946 by Alfred A. Knopf Inc. Reprinted by permission of the publisher. From *What I Believe* by Bertrand Russell. Copyright 1925 by E.P. Dutton, renewed 1953 by Bertrand Russell. Used by permission of Dutton Signet, a division of Penguin Books USA Inc. From Eugène Ionesco: *Journal en miettes, (Fragments of a Journal)* © Mercure de France, 1967.

Cover illustration: Arnold Boecklin. *Isle of the Dead.*
Museum der Bildenden Kuenste, Leipzig, Germany.
Transparency provided by Erich Lessing/Art Resource, NY.

Open Court Publishing Company is a division of Carus Publishing Company.

Copyright © 1996 by Carus Publishing Company.

First printing 1996

Printed and bound in the United States of America.

Library of Congress Cataloging-in-Publication Data

Fingarette, Herbert
    Death : philosophical soundings / Herbert Fingarette
        p.   cm
    Includes index.
    ISBN 0–8126–9329–9 (cloth. : alk. paper). --ISBN 0-8126-9330-2
(pbk. : alk. paper)
        1. Death. I. Title.
    BD444.F53 1996
    128'.5--dc20   96-42972
                                                                         CIP

for Leslie and Ann
with whom this silent conversation was held
and in memory of
Phil
with whom it was the last

CONTENTS

Contents

PART ONE

THE MEANING OF DEATH

What Is There to Be Explored?

1

Death as the Mirror Image of Life

True, death itself is nothing; but the thought of it is like a mirror. A mirror, too, is empty, without content, yet it reflects us back to ourself in a reverse image. To try to contemplate the meaning of my death is in fact to reveal to myself the meaning of my life. In this connection I think of one of the most powerful attempts to probe the meaning of one's own death, Tolstoy's story "The Death of Ivan Ilyich."

Initially, Ivan Ilyich reacts to the possibility of impending death in a way that I suspect most of us do: with denial. Maybe, he thinks, this isn't death after all. Maybe this pain is merely the effect of some malfunctioning organ. The doctors can probably put it right. Ivan Ilyich soon realizes these hopes are feeble straws. But he's impelled to grasp at them, impelled to continue hoping. He clings desperately to any sign that this is not *It*.

The final phase of the story begins when at last the evident futility of the doctors and his increasing suffering compel Ivan Ilyich to confront his terror. The confrontation begins abruptly. A voice within him suddenly speaks and asks: "What do I want?"

"To live," he answers instantly.

"How do you want to live?"

"Pleasantly, as before."

This inner dialogue leads Ivan Ilyich to a re-examination of his life, to review the "pleasures" he has lived for. He had seen himself as a cultured, dignified, and useful public servant of high rank, enjoying all the civilized pleasures such a life affords. Self-deception. Now he sees that his life has been an increasing commitment to a polite but mean-spirited and selfish inhumanity. He has evaded humane contact—and the obligations that go with it—by means of continuous, but burdensome, role-playing. He has enjoyed exercising power with "justice"—that is, without compassion. Facing death, Ivan Ilyich comes to understand the truth of his life.

What strikes me here is not the particulars of Ivan's way of life. It is the fact that his "confrontation with death" turns out to be a retrospective exploration and revelation to him of the meaning of his life. Seeing the truth of his life, he is able at last to face death and see its truth. At the end, the dying Ivan Ilyich asks himself, "Where is it?" "What death?"

Tolstoy answers, "There was no fear because there was no death."

Tolstoy probably had in the back of his mind a religious theory to account for "There was no death." We know the total Christian commitment that came to dominate his life. Still the story itself carries its own independent truth. The story merely announces the facts: The confrontation with death is in fact a confrontation of life; death itself has no meaning. The "fear of death" is in reality an agony that concerns life. The subjective truth that "there is no death" is not a statement about immortality, not an objective assertion contradicting the objective truth of death. It is a way of expressing the point that so far as anything I can experience is concerned—one might say, from the standpoint of the soul—there is no meaning to "my death."

There is a truth in this that bears reflection, a subjective truth: I, this consciousness, will never know death first hand. In the end, I'm invulnerable. From the subjective point of view my deepest wish is guaranteed—I am immune to death. ('Death,' said the philosopher Ludwig Wittgenstein, "is not an event in life; we do not live to experience death.")

Of course, I feel the logical strain such comments induce. The temptation is to return to "common sense," to be objective, "realistic," to face the plain truth that I'll die. This commonsense reaction, though objectively true, obscures the inner truth as I live it. The inner truth that I live is that my death will not be an event in my life.

I think it's fair to put things this way: There are two absolutely certain facts about this existence. From the objective point of view I am mortal—it is certain that I will die. From the subjective point of view I am immortal—it is certain that I will never die. Or to put it slightly differently: Never in my life will I experience death.

Obviously the immortality of which I speak is not the everlasting afterlife promised by some religious doctrines. It's a simpler, secular thesis. It's just the undeniable truth that I will never know an end to my life, this life of mine right here on earth.

This truth is for me the ultimate truth. For it is my consciousness, my subjectivity, rather than my body, that is to me my very existence, my existential identity, *me* as I most intimately know myself. I am not alone in this. The idea that one's consciousness could continue to live in some form even after the body dies is an idea that has ubiquitous and enormous appeal among human beings everywhere. The belief is false, but its appeal attests to the fact that the supreme subjective value is the life of consciousness, not the life of the body.

So people desperately hope never to know the end of consciousness. But why merely hope? It's a certainty. They never will!

So then if my being dead is a concept with no meaning subjectively, what do I have in mind when I think I'm confronting the idea of my death? If I'm confronting anything at all, it must be something in my life. In fact what it turns out to be is a vivid, imaginative capturing of what life is for me now, what my life has been—and most importantly, what it may yet be. It is an experience that tears through the veil of routine, awakens me from the complacency of taking life for granted.

Even when unexpected and spontaneous, the apprehension of death transforms the moment, be it the sound of my wife in the kitchen, or sitting at work in my study, or turning to watch dawn arrive. This momentary apprehension of an eventual end to my life, insofar as it has any imaginable content, is in fact an appreciation, a clearer, brighter vision, of what is here and now. I may recall glowing—or terrorful—moments in my past, or envision the life I have been aiming toward. In any case it's my life I'm exploring, appreciating. I cannot imagine death itself.

Why, one may ask, should it be important to *imagine* being dead? Obviously, I can't imagine what it is to be dead, since being dead is total non-existence. But there are a lot of things that I know are so and yet can't imagine. Why isn't it enough just to think about it, to describe to myself its nature?

The answer lies in the fact that imagination is the only way one can get the "feel" and grasp the inner significance of some past or possible experience. Thought alone is abstract, verbal, not experiential. The only alternative to imagination is actual experience. Actual experience is, of course, limited to the here and now. Tenuous and imperfect though it may be, the vicarious experience afforded by imagination—whether through memories or projection of possibilities—is the only way to experience what the future would feel like, or to recall the feel of the past.

I think of a trip we were planning to make to Paris. We lived there quite some years ago, but haven't been back recently. Should we make the trip? We try to picture (imagine) what it would be like for us under the conditions as we now understand them. Our travel agent says it's very congested. At first we are inclined to dismiss this: "That's true everywhere." But now we call up recollections—we imagine what it would feel like to be in our old leisurely neighborhood, a neighborhood we now picture as jammed with traffic and supermarkets. To imagine being there under those conditions is to find the vicarious experience displeasing. It is imagination that gives us the flavor of reality, and that is the basis on which we make our choice.

Yes, tenuous and imperfect, nevertheless imagining is genuinely a form of experience. One reacts directly to what one is imagining—not merely in thought but also in emotion and feeling, though in lesser degree than when actually experiencing it. I can *think* coolly about the possibility of my being in an auto accident. I buy insurance; I wear my safety belt. But if I truly imagine myself being in an accident I feel a kind of vicarious quiver of terror.

Imagining can also be viewed as a kind of role-playing. If I genuinely imagine myself walking down the street, it's a form of mental role-playing. I'm imagining I *am* walking; I'm imaginatively doing it. I imagine it as one of our long walks, and so I *feel* tired. At least I'm having some of that feeling if I'm successfully imagining it. If I don't feel it at all, then I'm not imagining doing it; I am at most thinking about it. It is one thing to know I will be tired if we walk. It is quite another to imagine myself as *being* tired.

Even when I imagine a scene where I'm absent, I'm playing the role of hidden observer, right there at that time and place. I "see" it happening right in front of me. If, for example, it's a horrible scene, and I'm genuinely imagining it, I actually have some of the same feeling of repulsion that I would have were I really there.

It is precisely because we can be engaged with a situation through the medium of imagination, even though not physically present, that we are emotionally involved in novels, films, dramas, stories. It is one thing to know the story—Desdemona is killed by Othello. It is a different matter to be emotionally, imaginatively gripped by the pathos and horror of it. Only if the story engages our imagination can we genuinely appreciate it.

So I come back to the sudden acute pang which arises when I contemplate my death. It must arise from confusion. I know that I'll be dead, but since I can't imagine being dead, I imagine, unwittingly, that I am conscious, a presence in that future world, conscious of it and yet utterly cut off from participation in it.

That way of imagining my "death" is confusion because in reality I would not be there to suffer such alienation and longing. Nevertheless, in its negative way, it does compel me to see and appreciate the people that mean much to me, the activities that fill my life, the true significance to me of the joys and the sufferings in my life. I am imaginatively living cut off from all this. The more imaginatively we confront "death," the more we are in fact envisioning, in the perspective of loss, the meaning to us of the people and activities that fill our life.

Of course, we also appreciate our life in positive ways. We thrust ourself into the things in this world that are of real value to us, into being and working with people, into activities we relish. A little while ago I was totally immersed in one of the late Beethoven piano sonatas, one of the sublimely beautiful offerings of this world. A few days before that I was completely caught up in play with my grandson: I played the villain, his mother was the princess, and he was the hero rescuing her from my clutches. We were all totally immersed, totally delighted.

On the other hand, I get a different, and important appreciation of life through the *via negativa,* the mirror image of life that death holds before me. This act of imagination shows the meaning to me of what I have by representing it as lost, wrenched away from me by death. It is in imagining their loss to me that even the trivia of daily life glow with a new radiance. Seeing life in the mirror of death is a revelatory experience.

There is the ancient teaching that tomorrow we die and so we should make the most of today. The paradox I saw in this teaching is that fear of death is not a motive that can engender truly carefree joy and fulfillment. Now I see the teaching from a somewhat different perspective. In recalling that tomorrow I may die, I discover, intensely illuminated, what it is today that makes my life full, that gives it meaning. That vivid revelation may enable me to live in a more focused way.

In this context I have new insight into an often mentioned puzzle. Why is it that my not having existed prior to birth causes me no distress, and yet the thought of my eventually ceasing to exist has such portentous meaning for me? The very question itself reveals that the mere fact of non-existence is not the issue. If it were, then we would feel the same about both periods of our personal non-existence. So there must be something at work here that goes beyond the mere matter of non-existence. Now I see what it is.

My relationship to the past before I was born is a matter of hearsay, not actual experience. I've read about, heard about, been taught about what happened. Whatever I may have learned and admired about the attractions of a Cleopatra or a Madame de Pompadour, I have never lived with them and loved them. Whatever the admiration I have for Jefferson, he was never a personal friend of mine.

The contrast is sharp when I imagine the post-mortem future, the future of people I've lived with, loved, disliked, respected, feared, dined with, worked with, fought with—the future of activities and projects into which I've put my heart. Suppose I do envision some situation where my wife and daughter are together, and I imagine they understand that I have died. They are sorrowful. While I don't imagine myself as present with them of course, still it's I who am doing the imagining, and so I react to the scene that is present to me. It's not a scene with people from history whom I've read about in books. I react to the sorrow of persons with whom I have had the most intimate relationships, the thought of whom inevitably arouses vivid memories, desires, hopes, and feelings of every kind.

The more powerfully I react to their relationships to me, the more intensely do I react to my imagined absence. It's akin to missing people in anticipation. I do that when I'm about to leave on a lengthy business trip. Even before leaving, I imagine being far away from home and I already feel longing for my wife and family. I may know that when the time comes I'll be so busy that I won't have time to miss them. That thought helps, but it doesn't by any means eliminate this feeling now. I am inevitably reacting *now* to what I *now* imagine, although I am imagining a future situation. To imagine my family at home and myself apart is to react by wanting to be there with them. It is imagined, but the feeling aroused is strong.

So the post-mortem future I imagine is the future of the life I'm living, though I imagine it going on without me. I "miss" all that has filled my life. The historical past I imagine is of a life I never lived. I don't miss any of these people or activities. I may wish I'd known them, but that's very different from missing people I have known and loved. No wonder I have the attitude I do to my prenatal past, which is empty of personal engagement. No wonder this differs so dramatically from my experience when I try to imagine my death. In the latter case it is a poignant experience rich with intimate meaning from the life I have lived.

Metaphors That Deceive

2

Separation, Sleep

Separation

𝒟eath as separation, as departure, is a familiar theme in folklore and literature. The French saying tells us, "Partir, c'est mourir un peu,"—to part is to die a bit. "Farewell," whether spoken to the dying or by the dying, is a theme that runs from Homer through Shakespeare to Keats and on into the present.

The theme of separation, and its profound impact on human beings of whatever time or place, is evident in the fact that in many societies the primary form of condign punishment is exile. In story and myth, and in personal memoirs, separation from one's people means incurable anguish.

Can one get close to the inner, subjective meaning of one's death by thinking of it as eternal separation? I have certainly imagined death as separation forever from my beloved wife, an intimate companion in my own great and trivial moments over many long years. This final separation seems a devastating prospect. My daughter also embodies a part of my life. To imagine departing forever from one so dear is to experience what is unnameably piercing to the heart. I will leave grandchildren, whose lives will move into youth and maturity, lives from which I will be forever cut off. Dear friends—lost forever. And then, too, there are the things in life that give pleasure or joy, or even transcendent beauty—music, literature, philosophy, the sun, the hills—gone. Does the shadow of death mean these things to me?

In my more sentimental moments I have imagined deathbed scenes. I suspect I'm not alone in this. I imagine myself saying "goodbye, goodbye forever" to those dearest to me. In a certain mood I imagine this vividly, concretely; and it becomes heart-wrenching.

Yet this is all confusion.

My death is not really a leave-taking, not really a "goodbye" situation *for me.* The notion of "goodbye" has surreptitiously taken on a radically different significance here from its normal meaning. Normally when I part from somebody—especially long-term, or permanently—the grief in parting consists in grief at the thought of living apart from that person. It has meant, I shall be without you. This implies I shall *be,* but without you.

With death, obviously, the situation is otherwise. I will not be at all. It will not be life for me apart from the person since there will not be life at all. After one's death there is no grief, no suffering, no sense of loss or separation. So to conceive of death as one's "goodbye" is confusion.

Nevertheless the force of lifelong habit fills in where imagination has no other option. One literally can't imagine what it will be like to be dead—there's nothing to imagine. What one does imagine is the nearest analogy—being separated from loved ones. Trying to imagine death, one unwittingly imagines something else instead, something that crucially misrepresents the matter.

This misrepresentation may reflect not only confusion but also a certain unconscious yet purposeful self-deception. To imagine myself separated from others is tacitly to deny my total non-existence. It's a self-deception in which I imagine a world wherein I am still alive, gazing, as it were, on my loved ones but, being "dead," I am unable to reach them in any way. This imaginative act is recognizable in the myth that the soul survives bodily death, externally separated from earthly affairs but still able to observe them. Thus the myth embodies the refusal to acknowledge one's eventual non-existence.

Of course, it's a different matter for one's survivors. They can say farewell in the same sense that we generally have in mind in parting forever from a loved one. They will remain alive. Theirs is the tragedy. Condolence should be for them. Their loss is genuine, their grief justified.

In my imaginary deathbed scene, I do grieve for those I leave behind. That's reasonable because, being still alive, I appreciate their grief, present and future. In my heart of hearts, however, an important element of the poignancy of this imagined scene is that I am also imagining it as if I were parting from them, as if it were my own loss, too. And that won't be true. I live no loss. I will never live apart from them.

Gabriel García Márquez writes of a dream he had, a dream that was seminal in a sequence of tales he worked at intermittently for several decades. He dreamed he was going to his own funeral, along with many of his young friends, all dressed in mourning, but all actually in a festive mood. As one of the group, he joined in the mood and the ceremony. When the services ended they all began to leave. So did he. But one of his friends stopped him and said, "No, *you* can't leave." In that moment, he says, he realized that "to be dead is to be with one's friends no more."

This dream represents the phenomenon I've been describing—the pathos of death mistakenly apprehended as an eternal separation from those one loves, from the vibrance of life itself.

Mistaken though it is to view death as separation, the mistake can be productive. To imagine being separated forever focuses the mind on how precious the people and the activities of our life are, and on how vulnerable we are.

There are some elements of comfort in the conclusions I've been reaching here, elements perhaps of false comfort. I have said that in regard to oneself death is nothing to grieve over since one won't exist. Is this *too* easy, too comforting? Is my reasoning here mired in its own subtle form of confusion and self-deception? It suggests that since I won't exist, and therefore won't be caring about my survivors, I needn't have any concern now about their welfare when I will have died. That can't be an acceptable conclusion.

Of course, it's true that the welfare of my sorrowing family won't matter to me when I'm dead. But it does and surely should matter now. My concern for their future welfare isn't based on the expectation of my own satisfaction in that postmortem future. There is satisfaction for me right now, life is more fulfilled for me right now, if I can think of them as faring well after my death. Surely such concern is part of what it means to love someone.

Then why wouldn't a similar logic apply to my own future welfare? Isn't it also rational for me to be at least as deeply concerned right now that I, too, should fare well in the future and not be dead? If one can rationally fear now for the future welfare of one's loved ones, why not for one's own future?

The analogy is valid. Certainly it's true that I'm justified in being concerned that I should fare well, not ill, in my own future. I'm justified, too, in my concern that my loved ones should fare well. But while faring well is one thing, and faring ill is another—being dead is quite a different ballgame. As far as death goes, the same holds in each case. Once the person is dead, be it myself or someone I love, why be concerned for that dead person? There is no longer any such person to fare either well or ill. Grief over the death of a loved one, if rational, has to do with one's own loss. There's no reason to grieve for the deceased. They don't suffer.

Someone we care for dies suddenly in the prime of life. What a tragedy! For *whom?* We answer instinctively: For the person who died. But why? That person suffers nothing. The tragedy is ours. We have lost what would have been a fruitful life. The thought makes us sad. But this comes from imagining a hypothetical future, a future that never was nor will be, but a future we wish would have been real. It is our loss. The person who is dead is suffering no loss. The fact is that there is no such person now. How can a non-existent person suffer loss?

It's a strange thing to anticipate my death as my being separated from my loved ones, since in the actual event I will not experience any separation whatsoever. I won't experience anything. I won't exist.

Sleep

We find similarities and also differences when we examine another age-old metaphor for death: Death as sleep.

Can this be what death in the end means to us—going to sleep? The durability of the metaphor is plain to see. "There she met sleep, the brother of death," says Homer. "To die, to sleep," says Hamlet. Shelley muses on the prospect that "death like sleep might steal on me."

The very self-evident aptness—and solace—of the metaphor induces one to overlook the important ways in which the metaphor is self-deceptive.

We have no word to describe the inner experience of falling asleep. I anticipate "falling asleep" while still awake; and on re-awakening I discover what happened. I do experience getting drowsy as the preliminary to falling asleep. Nevertheless, we are never aware of the actual happening, the moment of falling asleep. What is it like, that transition from being awake to being asleep? There is only one correct answer: nothing. What is it like, subjectively, being in dreamless sleep? Nothing.

This point can be generalized to all the ways in which consciousness disappears, whether from sleep, fainting, anaesthesia, or death. These, by their very nature, do not feel *like* anything because neither the transition nor the condition is an experience. It happens, but it's not experienced. It consists in the cessation of experience. In this rather strange and important way, sleep and death are surely alike. So dying is like falling into a dreamless sleep. However the two are radically unlike in the very obvious respect that we awake from sleep but never from death.

Why do these obvious features of sleep and death merit explicit attention? Because the metaphor of death as sleep is a comforting one. The point of the metaphor is that one should see death as welcome relief rather than feared catastrophe. After all, sleep is normally followed by awakening refreshed. The overtones of the concept of "sleep" are almost all positive and pleasurable. Death, too, may put an end to fatigue or suffering. But since there is no awakening, much less awakening refreshed, the picture changes radically. It is in this way that the intended comfort of the death/sleep metaphor turns out to be false comfort.

In the end, what is it that we seek comfort for?—certainly not for the mere absence of consciousness. Deep sleep and anaesthesia show that there is nothing momentous about mere non-consciousness. However the prospect of death, unlike sleep, signals the cessation of consciousness for evermore. So it is not the prospect of non-consciousness in and of itself that is potentially threatening but the question of what came before and what will come after. In this respect sleep and death are radically unlike, and the metaphor of death as sleep becomes deceptive.

3

Immortality, Selflessness

Immortality

Should one call the idea of an afterlife, of an immortal soul, an image that reveals the meaning of death? I see it, rather, as an image that denies death. Some form of this denial of death is ubiquitous among human cultures. Souls, spirits, ghosts—these are among the mythic notions that embody this idea.

The idea of immortality is characteristically embedded in a larger mythic or theological context. In Christian theologies, for example, bodily death is a portentous event. The soul leaves the body forever and begins an eternal spiritual life. The quality of that life is determined by the Divine judgment of one's earthly sins and merits. However, in Asian reincarnation doctrines death takes on a radically different meaning. It is the moment when the soul casts off the old body, as we cast off an old garment, and takes on a new body and a new life on earth. The moral character of one's conduct in earlier lives determines one's moral fate in the current life, but the current life is in turn a chance to shape future lives. Each different mythic and theological doctrine has its effect in shaping the distinctive culture to which it belongs. But in spite of their notable differences, each doctrine in one way or another denies death as a final end by centering around a doctrine of immortality.

Much as I wish I could believe some such doctrine, I cannot honestly tell myself that I do. There is no doubt in my mind that, if taken literally, such doctrines are not only false but are incoherent. The idea of a non-bodily consciousness such as the soul makes no sense because it is our physical being that locates us in time and space. For this reason all such doctrines are compelled to reify the soul"—to give it, in short, a kind of quasi-body, and thus a location in space and time. The soul is conceived as an ethereal kind of matter located at some point in space (or in Heavenly space). Or it is conceived as a ghost-like entity. It has to be located in space because this ethereal entity presumably sees and hears—and how could "seeing" and "hearing" make sense unless the one who sees and hears is located at some place in space? (What would a tree or a human being look like as seen from nowhere, or as seen from no particular point in time? Does a voice sound near or far, loud or soft, to one who has no physical location in relation to the speaker?)

For these and many other reasons one of the basic presuppositions on which all my thinking rests is that death is the end. There is no "afterlife," except in the sense in which the memory of me and of my objective achievements remains for those who survive me.

Selflessness

*T*here is a way of dealing with one's death that denies death its sting while not denying its reality. It is central to the major teachings of the East, but also has an important place in Western thought. It is the quest for "selflessness."

Many Eastern doctrines, and some Christian sects, attempt to remove the sense of self. The logic is easy to see: If one were truly selfless, what would be lost when death comes?—nothing. Or at least nothing of momentous importance. Death would not be seen as a negation of life—at least not a negation of one-*self*.

Yet the goal of selflessness goes against the grain of the modern Westerner. Our grand aim is self-fulfillment rather than self-abnegation. It's true that in the Judeo-Christian tradition there is a teaching of selflessness: Thy Will, not mine, be done. But as a practical matter, and especially since the nineteenth century, this teaching has widely been abandoned and replaced by assertion and even glorification of the self. Emphasis on the rights, the talents, the ambitions, and the achievements of the individual has become the hallmark of modern Western cultures.

This Western attitude contrasts sharply with the major Eastern teachings—Hinduism, Buddhism, Confucianism, and Taoism. These share the idea that the individual self is the major obstacle to the freeing of the spirit. The individual self is seen as a mere delusion or impediment to be dispelled by one or another means. It is an intrusive element that is the source of failure in human effort and of disruption in Nature. In the East it is self-evident that the achievement of selflessness is liberation from fear of death. Even Confucius, who enjoins us to "cultivate the self," actually means that we should seek perfection in properly living our social role and status. He clearly opposes cultivating our personal, ego-motivated appetites.

The idea of selflessness is easily misunderstood and then unfairly condemned. To many people "selflessness" is equated with asceticism, and indeed in Asia it is regarded that way by some sects. But that equation need not hold true.

Suppose, for example, that I am completely taken up in playing a piece of music. I "lose myself" in it. My self disappears. This is a form of selflessness, but it is also self-fulfillment, not asceticism. If I'm totally absorbed in the proper execution of some significant task, perhaps writing a book that means much to me, I lose my self in it. This, too, is self-fulfillment. If I find joy in promoting the success or happiness of some other person, my attitude can be equally well characterized as selfless or as that of a caring self. Such an attitude would be selfless in the sense that my central aim is not my own personal gratification or profit, but the integrity of the action itself. I simply want to do "what should be done' (to use the language of the Bhagavad Gita). Yet this caring act is done joyously and is self-fulfilling.

As an ideal, selflessness is not utopian. We've all acted selflessly at times. Surely I can nourish and encourage this attitude in myself so that it increasingly fills my life. I would like to think it's true of a portion of my life already. To a great extent I do surrender myself to my love for my wife, my daughter, my grandsons, to my work, to my music.

The achievement of selflessness brings with it a kind of liberation. To the degree that this is one's stance in life, death would be, as Marcus Aurelius said long ago, merely a natural event, not necessarily welcome but certainly not ominous. The less concerned with oneself, the less can the end of the self loom as a personal threat. One is free from the anguish peculiar to those who must defend their ego. Candor requires me to confess my limits: Though selflessness might be a valid ideal, I don't see myself fully reaching that ideal in reality. Perhaps with a different upbringing—maybe in a family where some tradition of devotion to intense spiritual discipline played a major role—I might aspire to such a condition of total selflessness. (Maybe only saints and yogins achieve it.) But the reality is that my life has been too Western, too secular, for me to entertain such an expectation seriously.

There is still another important obstacle to a totally selfless life. Hindu, Buddhist, and some versions of the Judeo-Christian teachings make a basic assumption that we today cannot honestly make. The assumption is that each of us has a definite God-given or fate-given destiny.

The Bhagavad Gita, for example, teaches that I must replace personal, self-ish aims, and devote my efforts to my dharma, the destined and proper station and role in life that I have been born into. I must be a good and faithful husband, father, and philosopher—or, as the case might be, a good farmer, craftsman, soldier, ruler. If we give ourself to service in our station in life, we are free from the anxieties of the ego-centered life. When death comes, it is the natural close to a life lived as destined. There is nothing to regret.

Something of the same kind is true of Confucius's teaching. He assumed that we could live fully and adequately if we faithfully and sincerely follow the customs, traditions, and ceremonies handed down to us. He never doubted their adequacy. And for many Jews and Christians, the sacred writings and authoritative commentaries lay down all one needs to know about how to live one's life.

In Taoism it is Nature which supposedly shows us the right road for all contingencies. The essential is to follow Nature and not interfere by intruding our ego and its personal aims. I do believe that we often intrude, disturbing Nature, imposing our own ego, our own preconceptions, rather than being open to what the situation calls for. We can learn much from Taoism's sermon against human meddling.

The modern vision, however, is of a world with bona fide options, with choices that are often unavoidable. We cannot accept the presupposition that Nature, or tradition, or Destiny" can decisively settle all questions for us. As we see it, choices are ineliminable from our world. So are the selves who must make those choices. The assumption of a world that presents us with complete answers for all occasions is not credible to modern Westerners.

In any case I know that total selflessness is not a practical option for me. That doesn't take away from the importance of achieving whatever degree of selflessness I can—and to that extent removing the terror aroused by that meaningless end of the self we call death.

I realize that what I need is an image of life and death that does not rely on supernaturalist evasions of the reality of death. I need an image that does not require the unacceptable assumptions about a fixed path for each of us that are built into the Eastern doctrines of pure selflessness. I need an image that does not misrepresent the true meaning of death by analogizing it, for example, to separation or to sleep. The image I seek would have to recognize the variety, the uncertainties, the vicissitudes of life. It would have to be an image for modern times—an honest one.

Metaphors That Enlighten

4

The World as My Life

What does my own death mean to me? It means the end of the world. Subjectively. Either something comes into my ken and is present to my consciousness, or it does not exist—at least not so far as *my* world goes. Subjectively I am the all-seeing center of the world. Subjectively, the focal point for all that is, all that might be, and all that ever was, is the conscious "I." This role needs to be explored here at greater length.

I am also, of course, an individual inhabitant of the world, but this role, too, is very special, indeed unique. While it's true that I am only one among the myriad other inhabitants of earth, I am acquainted with myself through a unique immediacy. I have a directness of insight into myself that is absolutely unavailable to anyone else. For example, others can observe the outward signs—my grimaces, my groans and gestures—of pain. That's objective. I don't have to observe signs that I am in pain. I just *am* in pain. I *feel* it; I don't infer it. For others my grimaces and groans are signs from which they infer my pain. For me they are *expression* of my pain.

Similarly with the control of my body: I am the only one in the world who can move my arm simply by intending that it should move. If others want my arm to move, they have to intervene physically, and even so they can't make my arm and hand do all the things I can. Nor can I do this with any other pair of arms in the world. So it's true that I am an inhabitant of the world along with myriads of others. But subjectively—from the perspective of my inner consciousness of my identity, and the way I control what I do—I am unique in the world, fundamentally different from all others.

With these preliminary remarks I can comment more fully on my role as the center, the observer of all, in the world that I know. For example, "the past" can have concrete meaning for me only insofar as I know about what happened or can recollect it from personal memory. Beyond this, "past" is just a word and no more.

To put the point more generally, anything at all that plays a role in the world as I inwardly live it is necessarily something that is present in some manner in my consciousness. If I am in no way conscious of it, then it's not in the world I *live*, the world of my experience. This is true not only of the past that I know, but also of the present and the future, of things in space, and in time, things I merely imagined.

Of course, I know that from the objective standpoint there are things of which I am not conscious. Indeed, we are so prone to give priority to what we take to be "objective" truth that we typically fail to explore the subjective world, the world as we actually experience it. The truth that I am the center of my world, the unique consciousness to which it is all present, is so obvious that I usually take it for granted and fail to appreciate its significance.

From this perspective, death plainly takes on momentous import. My death means more than just the death of one inhabitant of the world. When I cease to be, that whole world that I live—its space, its time and all they contain—disappears.

Although what I'm describing should not be confused with egoism, it is a deep source of egoism. In its egoistic form it reveals itself from earliest infancy. I remember when my eleven-year-old grandson went to France for a couple of weeks, and left his two-year-old brother behind. The two were very close. We all thought of the little boy as greatly missing his big brother. We were startled when the first phone call came from France, and the two-year-old refused to talk to his brother.

Instead he reacted with visible fury, crying "Andrew not my friend." It dawned on us that—of course—John was angry at his brother for having abandoned him! At two years of age, there was one world, John's world, and one inhabitant of prime importance in that world. The only relevant and understandable aspect of his brother's departure was that "Andrew left me!"

It's not uncommon to see a similar reaction even in older children when a parent dies. The rational adult sees the death as obviously involuntary, an occasion for grief. For the child there normally is grief, but close observers commonly report that there also is usually a deep anger, a resentment that can persist, at least below the surface, into adulthood. The event is perceived by the child in the perspective of the world as there-for-me. The death of the parent is experienced as abandonment. At that age, everything that happens is inwardly viewed as referring to me: What I want is what the world ought to give me.

Even in mature years, along with more realistic reactions, this ego reaction persists. Inexplicably to others, the newly widowed spouse may feel anger—and perhaps be candid enough to express anger—at the departed spouse for having died. The departed one may be blamed for some fatal carelessness without which death supposedly would not have occurred. This reaction is often so at odds with what seems a rational response to the situation that it commonly is suppressed except in moments of inward candor. It reflects the return under great emotional stress of a more primitive feeling: Death is an abandonment, unfair. It is experienced as done-to-me rather than as merely something that happened-to-the-spouse.

The situations I've mentioned up to this point illustrate the way in which one's centrality is manifest as a form of egoism. Such egoism, however, is not a necessary result of each of us being the center of the world. In speaking of myself as center, I have in mind something more fundamental, something that is inherently true of consciousness even without egoism.

When I say I am the center of the world, I'm describing a fundamental reality, not making a moral judgment or noting a psychological trait. Egoists are interested only in themselves, saints are interested in others and not themselves. I personally confess to having interests of both kinds. None of this changes the fact that each of us is the center of our own world, the consciousness to whom the lived world is present.

The point can be put this way. The history of my world may not always be *about* me, but it has been a history *for* me.

This way of putting things seems to clash with the common sense, objective truth that there's more to the world than I am conscious of. But subjectively, in the world as I experience it, this objective truth conveys almost no meaning. From the subjective standpoint, all it says to me is that in addition to what I've been conscious of, there's "more". What more? Well, if I could say what more I'd have to be conscious of it. "More" refers here to what I'm *not* conscious of. So "more," if it is to have any meaning at all, can only mean that this world of mine will always have further novelty, I know not what.

One might object: Aren't there things totally unknown to us that do have an impact on our experienced world? For example, what about those secret microscopic, organic processes that cause my present mood? These processes involve the workings of genes, of hormones, of many complex inner bodily processes of which I have no consciousness. They shape my conscious mood.

The answer has two elements. My mood itself is a subjective reality—I am conscious of it, I "have" it, whereas others can only observe my mood. My mood is present in my consciousness, even if only as its background or coloration. But what about the genes? My *knowledge* of them is also part of my subjective experience. If I knew nothing at all of them—as has been the case with most human beings in the history of our species—they would not exist in *my* world. They would have been part of that "more," an unknown cause of what I experienced. There are many things that I experience but whose secret causes I do not know. To say there are "unknown causes" is a way of expressing the fact that I do not always know why my subjective world is what it is. True, but uninformative.

Up to this point, in speaking of the inner self as the center of the world, as the consciousness to whom all is present, I have put the matter in language that suggested a largely passive relationship. Mainly I have spoken of our consciousness of the world as if consciousness were a kind of inner eye to which the passing show is visible. This image is profoundly incomplete. It fails to suggest how one's consciousness penetrates one's world, is diffused throughout it, in good part creates it. There are several ways in which this is so.

I screen what is allowed into in my world. I notice—become conscious of—the things that touch my interests, my likes and dislikes, my knowledge, my experience. I don't notice, and thus don't become conscious of the things that have no interest for me, or about which I know nothing. The architect, for example, has a knowledgeable interest in—and therefore sees—specific forms of building structures, designs, styles, traditions. Since I know little or nothing about architecture, I merely see "the building where my office is." The misanthrope notices the cruelty in the world, and that "evidence" strengthens his misanthropy. On the other hand the humanist's attention settles upon instances of heroism, compassion, and altruism, and so her world is populated with a very different sort of human race. I was surprised and impressed some years ago to realize that the shadows I see in a stereotyped way as always and entirely black are seen by the artist to have color. When I became aware that shadows could have color, this knowledge led me to see the colors of shadows.

There is a still deeper sense in which my world is mine: I not only screen items into or out of my consciousness, I actively create my world. My values, attitudes, concerns—these all give shape and color to whatever I perceive. Being devoted to classical music and to certain social values, I listen to rap music and hear it as harsh, repellent. Yet for many young people rap music has an exciting and provocative sound. They really do hear something different from what I hear. One might say: We hear the same sounds, but different music. We know the lover sees a special beauty in the face that others see as quite ordinary. So, too, seeing my awkward sketches, my little grandson was impressed and told me, "In my opinion, you're a great artist."

Suppose one could somehow be conscious of this world in the way a Turkish peasant, or an Aztec, or young inner-city gang member were conscious of it. I suspect one would hardly recognize it as the same world one had been living in. We look at the world and unwittingly we put so much of our self into it. The verb "live" should be used here as a transitive verb: We live our life and we also *live* our world. Our invisible presence is actively projected into the very nature of everything of which we're conscious. The world as I live it is in good part born of me, my creature.

It follows that to glimpse the end of one's world is not to glimpse something that is simply external to us. One's death is both personal and cosmic. This way of seeing things does seem to correspond both to the depth and the spontaneous character of the anguish that I feel when something happens that triggers the vivid thought: *The* time may have come.

And yet . . . . To attempt to imagine the end of this world is literally to imagine nothing. No more than one can imagine oneself being dead, can one imagine the non-existence of this world. One can imagine the *process* of dying, or imagine some cinema version of a world going up in a vast mushroom cloud. But it's the prospect of the actual end result—non-existence—not the process leading to it that evokes the distinctive anguish about death and the end of my world. Since this actual end is by definition a state of nothing, we are back to a new version of the old question: What can we possibly be imagining when we think of ourselves as imagining that our world has ended? What can we possibly be imagining when we imagine our non-existence? There is nothing to imagine. So what can it be that one could fear? What can one be imagining?

Could I imagine this familiar world continuing in existence even though I no longer exist? If I tried, it would be a world *imagined by me*. In other words, the world I imagine is the object of my consciousness, even though I'm not imagining myself as one of the inhabitants inside it. Yes, I can imagine a world without me in it as an inhabitant. But I can't imagine a world as unimagined by me. My consciousness of that world is ineliminable, and so, too, therefore, is my reaction to it. But this falsifies the meaning of my death, since its distinctive feature is that there won't be consciousness of, or reaction to, anything whatsoever.

When some other person dies, no matter how close, no matter how piercing the grief, the world (my world) still goes on. The rude truth is that *I* remain alive. The loss may be so grievous as to darken or undermine all life thereafter. Indeed my wife's or my daughter's life is so precious to me that were it necessary I'd give my life in order to have them live, or be freed of suffering, if somehow my death itself were needed to achieve that end. So the difference between the value I place on my life and on others is not a matter of a difference in importance; it's a matter of a unique *kind* of importance. My life can't have this unique kind of importance to anyone else.

Why can't we come to terms and be at peace with the fact that the prospect of death and the end of our world is simply the prospect of literally nothing at all? Isn't that the rational attitude?

The answer, I think, lies somewhere in the sources of a nagging anguish that won't be suppressed by rational argument. Considering that this world is so much my creation, so much an extension of me, the prospect of my end seems more momentous and anguishing than ever. How can that prospect not induce profound despair? Is the logic at fault?

And paradoxically, what can I make of that other utterly contrasting view of myself, the view of myself as a merely submicroscopic particle in the great scheme of things? There is a certain eerie feeling when I think about the amazing accident that I was born into life. It's much the same eerie feeling I have when thinking of the trivial changes of circumstance that could have meant my wife might never have been, or that my daughter, the daughter I actually have and love, might never have come to be. I reflect on the utterly accidental nature of our existence, on the unplannable, uncontrollable, unpredictable character of the fact that there happen to exist these particular individuals and not others, that in the course of our life we have run into these particular life situations rather than any of the infinitely many variations on them that might have come to be. Appreciating this, I appreciate how little that is fundamental in my life and my world has been in my power.

From this perspective I see that when I die there will hardly be a ripple in the great ocean of existence. Others will live, and more importantly, almost all will go about their business, my death having occasioned the most momentary of minor interruptions. There may be a memorial service. There will be some appropriate, often sincere remarks of regret. A minor punctuation in the rhythm of life for others—and then life will easily roll on as before. Will there subsequently, on rare occasions, be a parenthetical mention of me? Perhaps.

For my dearest ones, there will be far deeper, more lasting feelings. Life may take on a different coloration, even a different pattern. Even so, there being life, life goes on. And since life means activity, projects, and interests, the scar tissue will gradually heal over the wound, not unnoticeable, occasionally painful, but by and large covering and protecting the wound. For those who live there is, in short, no way to live except by living. Let the dead bury the dead. The others will in turn pass, and then even the memories of my presence will have dissipated into nothingness.

So my life, in the not so long run, is literally without consequence. How can I take it so seriously? Should I? The center of the world! Ridiculous!

Yet it's true that from a different angle I *am* the center of the world, the author and audience for all that is. The continued existence of my consciousness is not merely a matter of psychological longing, it's strictly inevitable. It's the essential condition that makes all meaningful existence possible. My central role is not just a matter of what I wish were so, it is a kind of logical necessity.

Oddly enough, whichever perspective I take—that I am the center, or that I am a fleck of dust in the cosmos—the implication is that in the end, I am alone. In our loneliness lies the meaning of our mortality in our life.

The loneliness of the human condition is a familiar theme. Poets and novelists have dealt with the theme. It is a platitude and yet a profound truth. No one can truly share my perspective on the world, no one else can feel my feelings, have my perceptions or my consciousness. They live *in* my world, but my world is mine, mine alone.

At least this loneliness is an aspect of the truth. Paradoxically, it's equally true, viewed from another angle, that there are those whose lives intimately intertwine with mine. A wife, a daughter, a brother, a friend, even a colleague of long standing—all share in one or another degree an intimacy with me. These intimacies are more than mere linkages; they are, as it were, interpenetrations. My wife is not merely someone I live with, do things with. We are literally part of each other's life. Intimacy is a kind of oneness. All this is reflected in those little trivial signs so familiar to intimates—thinking the same thing at the same moment with not a word having been said about it, knowing instinctively what the other will think, say, or do on a particular occasion. So I'm not alone—that's also a profound truth of my life.

Yet the prospect of my death elicits this awareness of being alone because no one else can die for me, and no one else dies by virtue of my dying. Moving toward my own death is my task alone. Others may stand near, may feel sorrow, may even be able to empathize with some of my feelings. They may feel with good reason that they are losing a part of themselves. Yet it is only a part, and for them the center remains.

This aloneness is one way in which one experiences being the center of the world.

The isolation we feel when we focus on this aloneness gains poignancy from our contrasting sense of the preciousness that comes from sharing life with others. To receive their understanding support, to know they stand with you, is to fulfill some primeval need within us. This sense of solidarity with others is one of the most precious things in life. Insofar as I feel alone, there's that inborn hunger to hear another voice, a voice whose very existence dispels the sense of isolation. Why do people keep the radio or TV on, even when engaged otherwise? To hear another human voice satisfies a deep hunger, quiets an undercurrent of disquiet. Silence is desolation.

Yet that is the silence one experiences when looking at the world from the standpoint of oneself either as unique center or as a speck in the cosmos. Either way, one experiences life in a way no other being can. One lives a life and a world that embraces others but that cannot, in the end, be shared. It's a strange, perplexing world where love is the proof that life can be shared, death the proof that it can't.

5

Life as Story

I have asked why I should be concerned about my death, since when that time comes there will be nothing distressing in it for me. It is illuminating to ask an analogous question about the eventual death of a character in a drama: How could the tragic hero's death loom as tragedy if he'll be dead and therefore he won't care? That seems a patently absurd question! But why?

Perhaps if I can identify what makes the question about the tragic hero's death so obviously misguided, I'll then be able to find an analogous confusion in the way I've put the question about my own death. There is certainly a strong analogy beteen a human life and a story or drama. It is worth exploring.

In a story, the Narrator, though invisible, is the unifying all-seeing consciousness. A story may be narrated in the third person, the storyteller not being a personage in the story. Even so, the Narrator-consciousness provides a unique perspective on the events. This is a perfect analogy to my consciousness as the unique, all embracing perspective on the world as I live it. Whether I am a participant or not, everything is seen through the lens of my consciousness. In a first-person narrative the Narrator is one inhabitant within the world of the narrative. Nevertheless, there is also present, though in the background and often unnoticed, the consciousness of the Narrator as storyteller. The analogy to my double status in real life is plain: I, too, am an inhabitant within my world, as well as being the unique consciousness that observes the whole of my world. Both I and the Narrator of a story observe the whole from a personal vantage point shared by no other being .

The end of the story is the end of the story-world and also of the Narrator-consciousness. When we come to the end of a story we may not notice this because, as in real life, we focus on the fate of the particular characters and the particular situations.

Of course, if it's a narrative told in the first person, it can't reach a definitive end. The character in the story who represents the Narrator can never be depicted as having died. So the end of that story, that world, can never be described. It simply stops at a certain point and no more is told. This is exactly analogous to real life: I can imagine my life proceeding to a certain point, but I can't imagine my life ending. I simply reach a point in imagining my life where I can go no further.

In a more literal sense, my world is my story. The structure of my world is not merely analogous to the structure of the story. The form in which my life has meaning to me is the same as in narrative. That is, I experience my life as a sequence of events in time related to persons, actions, emotions, intentions, hopes, fears. These are the elements of narrative, too—unlike, for example, the terms in which we understand physics, or biology, or mathematics. I experience and understand what is going on in my life in exactly the same terms as I understand a story. For this reason stories fascinate us in a way chemical equations don't.

My consciousness of the world, like the Narrator-consciousness of a story, plays a key role in establishing what tone and rhythm, what themes will dominate. I strive to make sense of things that people do. What does it mean—"to make sense of life"? It simply means fitting the elements into what I consider to be a coherent narrative. That is what the Narrator of a story does, but with vastly greater freedom (and skill) than I have in real life.

The story of my real life is not a neatly crafted story, not an aesthetically unified, coherent novel or drama; it's something of a hodge-podge. It's full of digression, overlapping subplots, unfinished lines of action, trivia, changes of style and tone, dull stretches. Yet insofar as it makes any sense at all, it can only do so as it makes narrative sense. No other format will do.

It is no accident that storytelling is ubiquitous and frequent among all humans. As imagined lives, stories offer a far richer repertoire of life-experience than a life without storytelling ever could.

A narrative does not have meaning by itself alone—it implies or presupposes a context, a world. The skeletal narrative or plot in a Jane Austen tale, for example, is coherent, but in and of itself has little interest. The plot includes a few rural gentry, their diffident misunderstandings, their genteel romances. It is the world in which they are set that one must appreciate in order to appreciate the story. For example, if this had been narrated by a popular sentimentalist writer of the day, the narrative would have been filled out in an archtypically penny-novel world of romance. As narrated in Jane Austen's way, the story presents us with a luminous world, resonant of humanity—a uniquely Jane Austen world. It's not merely that she tells the story better. In the penny romance, the Miss Bates of Austen's novel *Emma* would have been a simple comic parody, a target of laughter and ridicule to entertain us. In Jane Austen's world, Miss Bates is a tender, vulnerable, well-meaning human being. We smile with affection at her bumbling, as we smile at the innocence of the child. Austen's consciousness pervades, colors, shapes the world in which the narrative exists. Entering that world, we also enter Austen's consciousness, though she is not a character in the story.

In his memoirs, the renowned Peruvian novelist, Mario Vargas Llosa, remarks that a close friend and literary mentor helped him to understand an essential characteristic of fiction: Fiction, said his friend, is the novelist's way of re-creating the world in his own image and likeness, of subtly recomposing it to agree with his secret appetites.

So let me look at myself as the Narrator of my story. Like most narrators, I'm usually merely an observer, invisible behind the scene. I read about things, hear about them, watch them on

TV, see them as I go about my daily routine. All this belongs to my world, the world I observe, the only world there is for me. On a small stage within this world I also step forward as an actor in it. As I follow the story of this world of mine, I am always, even if unwittingly, looking at myself. This is highlighted by the fact that *your* story, in the very same time and place, with many elements similar to mine, is nevertheless told differently, and may even be in radical conflict with mine. How many are the novels, the court trials, the everyday situations in which one person says, "This is what happened," and someone else says, "That's not the way I saw it!"

We can try to make our world somewhat visible to others. It's not easy, but if I tell my story well enough to you, this may enable you to get a glimpse of my world. Not being a Jane Austen, my attempts are imperfect. Therein lies our endemic miscommunication with each other. There would be no miscommunication if we really were all living the same story, or if at least we were all Jane Austens.

A major difference—though one of degree—is that the storyteller has more freedom to control the course of events than I do in my life. Herein, of course, lies the source of the storyteller's power: The story can be shaped and made coherent, the central features can be intensified, made richer and freed of the extraneous. Yet I, too, have some control over my own life; whereas the storyteller's hand is often forced by the way the characters impose themselves regardless of the original plan.

I speak of myself as author and narrator. But what I've said implies that I am also audience, *the* unique audience for the story of my life . I have always been the audience, the ever present primary audience for what happens. I can only impute seeing and hearing to others, something I do on the basis of what I see and hear. But I don't impute the seeing and hearing to myself. I simply *see* and *hear.* In this sense I am unique in my world, the only audience directly seeing the show. All the others are part of a stage "audience" whom I observe. It's no puzzle for me that *they* can disappear from the stage. But like the real audience of a story or play, *I* don't disappear when the players leave the stage or when their story ends.

The story-life analogy is a rich one. Indeed in so many ways it is more an identity in kind rather than mere analogy. Having seen this in general, I can now draw the lesson relevant to my question at the outset: Why should the prospect of the tragic hero's death loom so ominously if, once he's dead, it won't bother him at all? I ask this question and presuppose that this audience reaction is exactly proper. If I can see *why* it is the sensible reaction, perhaps I'll then be able to answer my analogous question: Why should I react so strongly to the prospect of my own death, given that it won't at all be a condition of distress?

First the drama: Why should Desdemona's death at Othello's hands be tragic, given that we know that her death is release from all suffering? How do we explain our reacting to the heroine's ultimate fate with a kind of anguish? Why not simply view it with tranquillity, knowing that when this world ends, when it's all over, the whole thing will simply cease to exist? These two viewpoints seem incompatible, and yet each seems plausible.

Actually, it's quite a familiar phenomenon that I should hold two such conflicting views of a situation at the same time. Reading a novel I may be emotionally gripped by the struggles of the persons in that novel, following them with suspense, concern, hope. At the same time I'm aware that this is fiction, that these people don't exist and the events never happened. So why should it be puzzling that even while death casts its shadow over my life, I also know that in the end it will cast no shadow at all?

Having said all this, I find that the analogy of the drama suggests a deeper answer to my question about the anguish over death even while knowing there will be no distress when I'm dead.

Consider, for example, Othello's expressions of passionate love for Desdemona. These would have a very different meaning and quality in Act II—they would radiate unalloyed elation if I foresaw the play's consummation in happy marriage. In the actual play, however, these same words and actions of Othello's resonate from the outset with doom and horror. We know that this love is precisely what is going to drive him to murderous jealousy. It's not that Othello's gestures are simply gestures of love, but the audience happens to know it will all end in despair. We perceive these as gestures of *tragic* love. Their present quality is already colored by what is to come. The quality of doom can't be divorced from the immediate dramatic reality. Indeed that's where the playwright's mastery lies—the ability to provide a setting which shows a love that already, but unwittingly, speaks its own doom. That doom must be a real presence on stage in Act I, not just knowledge in the minds of the audience.

In short, the tragedy is not something that occurs at the end as the curtain comes down. The tragedy lies in the movement toward that end, beginning with Act I. It is a tragic play, not merely a play with a tragic ending.

All this suggests that the question I have to ask is not, What *will* my death mean to me when it happens? (Simple answer: Nothing.) The proper question is, What does my future death *now* mean in my life? Caught up as I am in the ongoing story of my life, engaged, involved, committed, how does all this have some distinctive quality and meaning for me now as I see it in the light of my mortality, in the future absolute end of the story?

These thoughts bring home to me how past, present, and future are all in the Present for me. Subjectively, my Present is not like one dot on the dotted line of time, a dot distinct from the dot that preceded it, distinct from the dot that will follow. On the contrary, this directly experienced moment flows without a break into the future, and it contains its past. What has already happened gives meaning and content to this Present; what is foreseen gives meaning and content to this Present.

What, then, is the specific meaning or quality that my foreseen future death contributes to my life now? What should I make of this life, given that it is a mortal life? I now understand the sense of this question better than I did. But that doesn't yet provide the answer. Here the analogy with tragedy breaks down. I can't honestly look forward to my death as the culminating moment of a classic tragedy, nor do I even know how the end will come. I'm not alone in this, of course, So what does the prospect of death mean or what should it mean in this present life? Many questions remain, though perhaps I've dispelled certain of my initial misconceptions and paradoxes.

6

Life as a Visit to Earth

Call it an image, a metaphor, or whatever. In any case, it seems to me apt to think of my life as a visit to earth. I arrive a stranger, without language, without understanding of this earthly world. Over time I learn something of the language, the ways of the people, some of their history. I join in their activities, even become intimate with a few. I get the feel of life on earth. The visit will have turned out—as visits do—to have not only its delights, but also its ordeals, its stretches of boredom or annoyance. Of course, being a visitor, my time here is limited. That has always been the idea.

It's a long, rich, and engaging visit when viewed in its own terms, but a brief and highly localized one when viewed in the perspective of the space and time of the world I've been visiting. I can see this visit as a lucky chance, a privilege—very limited, to be sure, but wonderful to have had at all.

What if I never saw this life on earth as anything but a visit? My whole mental set when I visit is different than when I think of myself as in permanent residence. Knowing—*feeling*—that the visit is to be for a limited time affects one's planning. It adds spice to the planning and to the activities themselves. We commonly regret leaving when a visit ends. Still, that end is not foreseen as an interruption or catastrophe. It is a natural closure, as integral a part of the visit as the departure from a dinner at a friend's.

Yes, comes the retort, but when you visit London, or dine at a friend's house, there's always home to go back to. When you die, you go nowhere. That's true. I came from non-existence; I'll return. That's not at all like going home. That's where a visit to a friend's and life as a visit to earth are poignantly different. Yet when I am on a visit that absorbs me, it's as if there were no past or future outside its bounds. I don't think about home and the routines of life there. I enjoy the here and now. It's total immersion. That's why a visit is liberating.

The image of the visit to earth can be easily elaborated. Some people go on a visit with the aim of doing and seeing everything possible. So the time limitation can introduce a note of desperation. In my view, the good tourist knows that one needs time for reflection, for rest, for rambling about the streets, as well as for periods of intensive and well planned activity. You can't see everything in one visit, so don't expect to "cover" everything.

The idea of the visit to earth does carry an overtone of alienation. If I'm a visitor, I'm not totally one with the people and the world that surround me. In the final analysis and in relation to all others, I am, as it were, alone, an outsider. That is an important virtue of this perspective on life. The metaphor embodies the idea that it's a mistake to identify oneself totally with this world. An element of alienation adds much that is valuable to life itself.

Alienation provides a detachment that cuts through parochial blindness. Having arrived in this world a visitor, I'm more readily struck not only by the oddities but also by the wonders of what I see. I'm not so inclined to take what's around me for granted the way natives do. I don't become blind to what should be seen, or bored by what should be fresh.

This does not amount to a dilettante approach to life. It's not the cynical attitude of one who smiles with condescending tolerance at the futility of wholehearted commitment. On the contrary, alienation is an essential element in authentic commitment Here I think of the commitment—and the alienation—so characteristic of the creative artist. To create is to see afresh and do what is new, to break the old molds and fashion new ones. No wonder the art of one's own time can be puzzling or threatening, or can simply seem absurd.

So, too, in a visit one can put oneself enthusiastically, wholeheartedly into the projects and doings, and yet still remain somehow apart. This combination of commitment and alienation enriches the experience. It can be exhilarating and in no way detached and cynical. We live something similar when playing a game with our child. To make it really work, we put ourselves wholly into it, a genuine participant, not a condescending adult. Yet this does not eliminate our adult detachment. Indeed the latter enhances the experience.

There is, an aspect of the visit that I've mentioned and passed quickly by, a feature that differentiates a visit from a human life. Although I may not explicitly think of it, in the back of my mind I am aware that life will continue after my visit ends. Obviously the same can't be said about that ending we call death.

Interestingly enough the Asian idea of reincarnation can be seen as an attempt to treat life as a visit, and to remove the difference between the end of a visit and the end of a life. According to reincarnation doctrine, when my visit to earth in this body is over—when I die—I, my soul, enters a new body, and begins a new life on earth. In this view I'm engaged in a seemingly endless (and wearying) round of visits to earth. This doctrine dominates Asian thought.

Unfortunately I can't believe in karmic rebirth as objective truth. I can't believe that I actually had previous lives in physical time or that I'll have subsequent physical lives in physical time. Life, for me, must be a single visit in which I arrive out of nowhere, and return to the same. And that's it.

Can I *really* see my life as a visit to earth? If I could, that would give a different color to life; it would redefine the significance of everything in life. In everything that I plan and do, in moments of friendship or intimacy, it would be my subliminal understanding that this is a visit, that my luggage is at the ready, that at some point I must pack up and go. All the more reason to make the most of it. All the more reason not to take myself and this life too seriously. In a visit this paradoxical double attitude is typical.

Am I being realistic? Or is this line of reflection an intellectual entertainment but no more?

In an effort to test the idea seriously, I have recently been recalling to mind this image of the visit, explicitly and with some frequency. Yet this takes effort. The difficulties I've encountered make it all the more evident how powerful a hold on me my former attitudes on life still have. It may have often been subliminal, but I can see how true it is that I have been governed all my life by the image of myself not as a mere visitor to the world but as its very center. The image of life as visit has at least provided a certain distance from which perspective I can examine more dispassionately my ego-centered attitude instead of being an unwitting captive to it.

This revelatory sense of contrast has popped up in curious ways. For example, on my actual visits to other countries it has happened on a number of occasions that my eye lit on some pedestrian rapidly walking by. I'm struck by her obviously intent, purposeful bearing. It suddenly becomes vividly real to me that the important thing in her life at this moment is the appointment to be kept, or the office to be reached, or the shopping to be done. My reaction is almost visceral: The center of the world for her has always been *there*, where she walks, in what she is doing. I have a sudden sense of myself as just an unnoticed pedestrian, a passing cipher populating her world with anonymous "people," exactly the same role she and innumerable other passers-by have played for me. She has been living her life—a childhood, youth, a marriage, a family—and this has been what her world has centered around. And I knew nothing of it!

The words on paper seem fatuous to me. They don't convey adequately this spontaneous, real, and powerful reaction. It's not that I acquired a new item of factual information but that I experienced an eerie, unsettling shift of perspective on the facts.

As I'm observing her, she momentarily turns her eyes to me. What is happening? I'm looking at her. No, I realize from that same unsettling shift of perspective that *she* is looking at me as I anonymously pass by and disappear from her world.

Of course, I'm interested in others in this world, not just in myself as the center. I've been truly concerned about the problems of the poor, the ill, the oppressed, here and abroad. I follow domestic politics and foreign affairs. I see pictures on the TV screen of suffering human beings, and I believe I feel genuine compassion. But these are, as it were, people in snapshots. These are not full blown personalities. I have no sense of the brothers or sisters of this individual, of what she ate for breakfast, if anything, of where and how and with what bodily pains she'll go to sleep tonight, of her personal friends and enemies, of what she'll be doing an hour from now, of a life being lived, a life and a world centered *there*.

Now that I am more self-conscious about the matter, such experiences make me realize vividly how central to my inner life has been the sense of the world revolving about me. Such experiences force me to acknowledge that my effort to see my life as a visit to earth is still a project, not a *fait accompli*.

It may seem that what I've been saying could be said without invoking the image of the visit to earth. It may seem I could simply say: We arrive here, and eventually we go. The "facts" of life, and certainly of death, are there for all to see. The Buddhist, the Jew, the Christian, the Stoic, the Homeric Greek warrior, the Trobriand Islander—all live in this same world, and all recognize the same basic facts of life. All can say we are as aware as you are of the transiency of life on earth, and we take account of it *in our own way*.

Yes, but the differences in the way the facts are accounted for is what makes all the difference. The images, metaphors, theories, and doctrines, in terms of which those facts are perceived portray different worlds and give different meanings to life and death.

Metaphors and theories have enormous power to shape different ways of life on the foundation of one and the same basic fact. This is evident in many areas of life. An example from another context may help bring out the point. Consider the "raw" fact of human suffering. Human suffering is ubiquitous.

However, the Buddha depicted suffering as the symptom of
spiritual disease, a disease whose causes he set forth, and whose
removal he declared to be the way to a cure. The diagnosis, eti-
ology, and cure as he taught them are what we know as Buddhism. All of this is no more than a metaphor based on the
notion of (bodily) disease. Yet the elaborations of this metaphor
shaped a culture.

Christians also see human suffering as ubiquitous, but they
see it as rooted in Free Will and Sin, rather than as sickness.
"Free Will" and "Sin" are metaphors by means of which everyday choices and common moral infractions are given a universal, metaphysical status and are declared to be the central chal-
lenges of life. This leads to a radically different attitude toward
suffering than does the "disease" metaphor. Sin calls for atonement, not a cure.

The Hindu sees suffering as *maya*, self-delusion. Neither a
cure for disease nor atonement for sin are the answer. What is
needed is knowledge or a discipline for living that will dispel the
sense of a personal self—a malign mirage that has most of us
hypnotized and deluded. The Jew sees the people's suffering as
God's test of the people's faith. Piety is the answer. The
Enlightenment thinker (and thus many a modern believer in
Reason and Progress) saw suffering as the effect of irrational
social institutions. The answer lay in what they thought was the
historically inevitable progress of Reason, with the consequent
rational reform of social institutions.

So the raw fact of human suffering is acknowledged by all.
It's the *image* that gives meaning to the fact, and thus transforms the meaning of life for believers in each doctrine.

And so it is with death, too: There is the Christian image,
the Islamic, the Jewish, the karmic image, the Confucian
image—in short, different images shaping different cultures but
arising out of the raw fact of death which belongs to human
nature everywhere.

For me the theological or supernatural doctrines, taken as
objective description, are beyond plausibility. And the Enlightenment's optimistic theories about human Reason are not credible.

As I see it, such objections do not apply to the metaphor of life as a visit to earth. This latter metaphor, if candidly seen as metaphor, seems to be both simple and apt That it is metaphor is no objection, provided I don't add an elaborate mythic over-lay designed to make it appear to be literal description.

Make the experiment, I tell myself. Make the experiment. Take it seriously. Imagine that right now you *are* on a visit. I feel the shift in attitude immediately. At least for the moment the difference is real. I feel a sense of liberation from anxiety about death—it *feels* more like the forthcoming end of a visit rather than the end of the world. I regain a certain excitement about the day ahead, a day of zest for exploration, of anticipatory pleasure.

I said to myself a moment ago *"Imagine* you are on a visit." Why do I say "imagine?" That's because the reality as I have always defined it for myself is my status as permanent resident. "Imagine" contrasts here with "really." But what if I were to establish as truly habitual the sense of my life as a visit? Then the "visit to earth" would not be "imagined." It would be for me the "reality." If that were so, how would I view the idea of my being a permanent resident of this world, even the center of it? Why, *that* would be imagination since it's obviously not a reality! Indeed, that would be to imagine patent fantasy.

Imagining can be a form of daydreaming—a condition that I begin to see I've been living in for much of my life. Perhaps there's something to the Hindu idea that life—as usually per-ceived—is a mirage, a daydream, a fantasy. It's not that this ego-centered perception of life is morally bad; it's a daydream from which I must fully awaken.

I can test the presence in myself of one or the other of these two ways of looking at my life in very practical ways. For exam-ple, when I confront the prospect of death in the way that induces that awful chill, that sense of soul-piercing termination, then plainly—whatever my intellectual position in the matter—my inward, subjective perspective on life locates me as the cen-ter, with an indefinitely extended future, with a natural right to continue.

Suppose, on the other hand, that my spontaneous reaction to seeing death ahead is not sudden shock, not a sense of doom. Suppose that I really have come to live each moment not as my due but as a limited privilege, a temporary opportunity to see a bit of life before leaving again. The great question is not how I meet death at the end, but the spirit in which I live each moment of life. That is what will determine what the end of life means. It is a question of the extent to which my inward attitude to my life is genuinely that of a visitor to earth. It's a test that doesn't lie. Would that I could consistently pass it!

Arriving at such an alternative vision of the basic meaning of my life is not simply a matter of arriving at a logical conclusion. Nor is it simply a matter of deciding to make the change. It's not like choosing to join the Smiths this evening rather than the Jones because I find the Smiths more interesting. Choosing an alternative vision of life is a matter of learning to see differently, to think differently, to live differently. It takes effort, discipline, constant rethinking, and time.

The old way of looking at life has a tenacious hold. Again and again I realize with a start that I've unwittingly slipped back into seeing things from my point of view as center of the world. Then I have to think my way through again to a genuine feel for myself as a visitor to earth, not the principal actor.

Have I arrived not at an end, but at a beginning?

7

The Ceremony of Life

When I have a vivid sense of death I feel an intense gratefulness for life. I feel how precious it is just to be able to sit at this desk, to hear the everyday sounds about the house. At such times I don't merely know it; I *feel* this moment of life as a gift.

But soon this vivid awareness dissipates. Within as little as a few minutes, and in spite of this insight, sitting down at my desk has already lost that precious quality, lost its aura, has become, once again, just the mechanical routine of sitting down at my desk. I still know I should be grateful for the moment, but it's not something I actually feel.

Why can't I hold on to that vision of the everyday? Why can't I actively appreciate the moment? Was the "insight" illusion? Or was it valid, and does the fact that so much of life seems routine simply show how insensitive I am to the wonder of life? Why doesn't that incandescent insight, if it's valid, transform my everyday consciousness?

I keep thinking and hoping that this momentary insight could stay with me so that I would live in a world continuously perfused by my thankfulness to be in it. These seem to be vain hopes. I quickly take life-as-usual for granted, as if it were mine by natural right.

As I see it, this sense of gratitude for life should be present even in the face of frustrations, irritations, and defeats. That lively sense of gratitude should keep all the frustrations in perspective. After all, the frustrations are part of being here, alive, with life ahead, rather than (chilling thought!) being gone forever from this world. The same holds equally true for the successes. Satisfaction in success should be tempered with humility, with the awareness that all this is a gift.

So my inability to sustain this sense of gratitude moves me to a kind of moral despair. I feel both frustration and guilt over the evanescence of the feeling of gratefulness. Is there an explanation for this failure—an explanation other than a dulled moral sensibility? Is there anything I can do about it?

So far as explanation of it goes, I think the answer lies in the general truth that feelings and emotions—I mean the actually felt reactions—are by nature transient. Feelings arise in reaction to a particular occasion, and they typically dissipate soon after the occasion. If the situation lasts long, the actual feelings will usually dissipate prior to the ending of the situation. Even when feelings are very strong, one calms down after a bit. Persistence of the actually felt emotion is relatively rare. Moreover, emotional reactions depend not only on the external situation to which we react, but also on our inner state at the moment. Being hungry I feel a surge of delight at the prospect of a fine dinner; but if I'm sated I have no such feeling. If I've had a bad day at the office I come home in a state that leaves me prone to react with anger to things that normally I'd ignore. Perhaps, if I'm to react to a situation with gratitude, there must be present some suitably receptive mood or need.

Could the feeling of gratitude be more like a mood than an emotion? There is no sharp boundary between emotions and moods—the emotion of anger may blend into an angry mood. Moods are more diffuse than emotions, less immediately tied to action. They are predispositions that can persist longer than emotions. Yet in the end moods, too, are transient. They vary, shift, and in the normal course of things dissipate in a matter of minutes or hours. It is the exception and often seen as abnormal if a person is persistently in a gloomy mood, or unremittingly sullen, or even in a constantly euphoric mood. Transiency seems the rule, be it mood or emotion.

This truth can be obscured when, for example, I can truly say: "I've never stopped feeling grateful to my friend ever since he helped me so generously years ago." This is a common and legitimate idiomatic usage of "feel." However, it obviously doesn't mean that ever since that time I have continuously had a conscious feeling of thankfulness to my friend. It's a way of saying that the fact of his help remains stored in my memory. It implies that I act appropriately in circumstances where that debt of gratitude is called upon. It suggests that on occasion some event or lively memory evokes the conscious thought of that generosity, and this in turn arouses an active feeling of gratefulness. Most of the time, however, I'm not having any actual feelings.

Maybe it's just impossible to be feeling actively grateful for each moment of life. It's a shame, but it's a fact that this wonderful and well justified feeling very often is absent. Would that human nature were different!

I have asked myself whether there is anything I can do that would be consistent with human nature, and that would also do more to keep such feelings alive. Is there some other route to a life more filled with active gratefulness?

I think there is. It starts from an idea currently very unfashionable in the contemporary West. However, the idea was central to the teaching of Confucius, and it still has force in the East. Confucius' vision of human life may be helpful to us because it compensates for a characteristic blindness from which we modern Westerners suffer—our blindness to the ceremonial dimension of social existence.

We have no one English word that quite captures the key Confucian idea. Nor for that matter did the Chinese language at the time—for Confucius' vision was genuinely novel even then. The key Chinese term he adopted was *li*, a term that at the time normally meant something like "rites," "ritual," or "ceremony." Confucius used it in a way that greatly enriched its meaning. He used it to serve his new vision of what it is that makes social life distinctively human.

In Confucius's lifetime, ritual and ceremony were too often merely façades, hypocritical gestures. They veiled a ruthlessly self-serving attitude toward social norms and traditions. War and greed were the order of the day. His contemporaries suffered from the same failure of vision that we do today: They saw custom, tradition, ceremony—the forms of civilized life—as mere surface decoration, as restrictive rather than liberating, as façades behind which to disguise the raw realities.

Confucius was not alone in recognizing this hypocrisy. His deeper, unique insight was that ceremony is not a mere decorative surface of life but the very structure that makes life truly human. And he saw that the exploitation of ceremony therefore corrupts the very essence of truly humane civilized life. "Ceremony" meant more to Confucius than the pomp and stylized conduct recognized as "a ceremony." His contribution was to show how ceremony, understood in its most general form, plays a crucial role in all the humble doings of everyday life. It is in this larger perspective that we see how the corruption of ceremony is the corruption of our humanity.

The gist of his meaning can be easily illustrated. Sometimes we welcome a guest to our home in an obviously formal and ceremonial way. Far more commonly, we need to give no more than a friendly, relaxed greeting. What we usually fail to notice is that even an "informal" friendly welcome is a ceremony, a conventionally prescribed symbolic form of action. We shake hands, smile, offer some words of welcome and of inquiry as to well-being. The occasion takes on a different meaning if any of these ritual acts is omitted. Ceremonies of welcome are universal, but the specific ceremonial forms used are conventional, traditional, peculiar to each culture. Americans shake hands, Europeans embrace, Japanese bow. Each of us has to learn the ceremonies of our group, or else pay the price in misunderstanding and awkward social relationships. What's more, if the ceremony is to be fully successful, it usually must be learned well enough to be performed with skill and spontaneity. If Westerners do not understand and haven't mastered the nuances of the Japanese bow of greeting, this will significantly affect the nature of the personal relationship entered into when Americans are greeted in Japan.

As the preceding remarks imply, the word "informal" can mislead. It does not mean an absence of ceremonial forms. It means that the ceremonial form does not call attention to itself as such. Or it can mean that some more traditional convention is symbolically rejected. Even so, the rejection is expressed in a ceremonial form if it is to have its intended meaning. For example, the current use of first names where formerly the use of last names was traditional is a mark of "informality." It is, of course, the new ceremonial form required if the intended personal relationship is to be established. A breach of this new form changes the tone and meaning of the relationship.

It is informal if one merely says "Hi, come in" to a friend who drops by. But the meaning of the occasion would change markedly if one simply opened the door without a word, turned one's back, and failed even to accompany the visitor into the house. Ceremony is crucial in giving meaning to human relationships.

We have an enormous repertoire and hierarchy of ritually meaningful gestures. Some are complex and stand out as "ceremonial," such as "formally" introducing one person to another, or offering a toast at a state banquet. Less obviously "ceremonial" is our arrival at work, when we give a conventional greeting to our co-workers. These greetings of "Good morning," or comments about the weather, commonly have no utilitarian function. They are ceremonial. But they are felt by all as the proper way to establish that the day's relationship is starting on a good footing. Their absence would be noticed and taken as a sign of something amiss.

Even when it comes to the animal need to ingest food, we don't eat as animals do. Each society has its ceremonial way of eating that transforms brute nourishment into a truly human form of social intercourse. Indeed some languages mark the difference by using different words for eating by animals and eating by human beings. Americans sit on chairs at tables and use knives and forks. The Chinese use chopsticks, and burp to show appreciation of the food. The tradition in India and in many other lands is to use hands and fingers to raise food to the mouth, but this is always done in some communally stylized "proper" way. There is no human community, whatever its size, location, or nature, without its eating ceremonies. When we see a family that eats on the run, separately, rather than dining together, we see the breakdown of certain profound human relationships.

Foreign cultures provide particularly clear examples of the role of ceremony. I remember back in the 1960s, when we were traveling in Austria, some young German women who had recently visited America expressed to me their incredulity and repugnance at the "animal-like" American practice of cramming a thick hamburger directly into the mouth rather than using a knife and fork. In German culture, at that time, it was not a recognized ceremonial form. It was, therefore, "animal-like."

And I remember realizing when we were in France that a smile in France has a different conventional meaning, and is appropriate in fewer social contexts, than in America. The result is that we misread each other: In certain contexts where Americans routinely and spontaneously smile, the French don't. Americans see the nonsmiling French as "cold," unwilling to establish a cordial humane relationship. And the French see Americans as smiling even when (in French custom) there's no occasion to smile. So the French see the forever smiling Americans as rather silly and childish, as amusing barbarians. Americans have an analogous misperception, in reverse, in relation to Japan. Young Japanese women frequently engage in a conventionally meaningful giggle, which to the American has no ceremonial meaning and therefore appears as silliness.

Ceremony has far richer nuances than we realize once we have mastered it and use it spontaneously. The tone of voice used in speaking to one's boss will not be appropriate in speaking to one's child. The intonations of speech to a male office colleague are not the same as used with one's fiancée or one's wife. A young man doesn't use the same tone of voice to his aged aunt as he does to his male companions. There is a way for a man to look at his fiancée when speaking to her and a way to look at his male professor when speaking to him. These tones of voice and forms of eye contact may differ in only subtle ways physically, but ceremonially, in their social meaning, they can make the difference between an effective social relationship and a disrupted one.

There are those who criticize ceremony as "useless," "nonfunctional." This hits the bull's-eye. It also misses the point. It's true, but that's precisely what's important about ceremonies: They are not utilitarian. Ceremony is what transforms the merely utilitarian into the distinctively human. It civilizes the human animal.

In Confucius's insight lies the key to my question as to how ceremony can play a role in enabling me to feel continuously grateful for my life. Since ceremony defines the meaning of the moment, the more I give it emphasis, the more it gives me a heightened consciousness of the moment and its meaning.

There is another respect in which ceremony can overcome the limitations I mentioned earlier about the transiency of feelings, and in particular the feeling of gratitude. Feelings and emotions, when independent of ceremony, are not only transient, they are involuntary. They are merely reactions to a situation, not actions subject to our will. Ceremony on the other hand is action. Being voluntary conduct, it is in our control. It reflects choice. I can utter at will the friendly words of greeting; I can offer at will the handshake, and smile if I wish. In this way I can at will provide a ceremonial framework in which I treat the occasion as one of friendliness and hospitality. Or I can choose to act otherwise, and then the feeling along with the meaning of the situation will be different. Ceremony, unlike emotion, is amenable to my purposes. By means of ceremony I elicit the pertinent emotions, moods, and feelings. Apart from ceremony, emotions and moods can only be reactions to circumstances, and thus independent of my will.

The answer to my question about sustaining the feeling of gratitude is implicit in the fact that ceremony evokes and embodies feeling. If I am spontaneously engaging in the forms of friendly welcome, I normally also *feel* friendly. Confucius wisely said: Ceremony without the feeling that belongs to it is not genuine ceremony. Thus acting with a heightened sense of ceremony means acting with heightened feeling as well. The ceremony gives the inner feeling outward shape and expression. The outer behavior evokes the feeling.

I realize now that what I seek is not so much the specific feeling of gratefulness but the heightening of feeling for the particular significance of the moment, whatever that significance may be. What I desire is emotional as well as intellectual appreciation of each moment for what it is. My mistake was to assume that what I should desire is one self-same feeling,— "gratitude"—persisting unchangingly throughout each day.

My grandfather was a devoutly religious man whose religion called for a specific prayer and ritual procedure for going about each new activity in the course of the day. As a nonbelieving youth, I thought this practice of giving each activity a ceremonial frame was archaic and an inordinate waste of time. Similarly, I was initially appalled at the great attention Confucius paid to the detail of the proper forms for almost every daily context and activity—dress, demeanor, speech, behavior. My reaction to Confucius recalled the reaction I had to my grandfather. Eventually, I came to understand Confucius's vision of the role of ceremony in life. Only then did I appreciate in retrospect my grandfather's ceremonial life.

We tend to be blind to the pervasiveness of ceremonies in our life precisely because we usually have mastered them well enough to use them spontaneously and with more or less adequate skill. So we take them for granted. Of course, skills vary, and some people are more socially adept than others because they have better mastery of the ceremonies—especially the subtler features of the ceremonies—that bind us together. Our blindness to this ubiquity of ceremony makes us think we modern Westerners are "liberated" from ceremony, and we tend to scorn it. Indeed we think of conventional forms as obstacles to human relationships. This is gross misperception, even self-deception.

We are familiar with the down side of ceremony. Social conventions, rituals, and ceremonies easily become stale routine and even oppressive. Preoccupation with rituals and conventions can result in emptying life of its vitality and producing a formalistic sterility.

That ceremony can become empty and stifling is not an objection to it, but a reason for thoughtfulness. Everything with a potential for good that we human beings do can also be perverted—that's the nature of the beast. In spite of the risk, we have to use our powers, fallible as they are, and as vulnerable to corruption as they are. We need constantly to be alert to our tendency to abuse whatever has a legitimate use. Ceremony is a case in point.

Confucius, too, saw that an obsession with forms, and the ignoring of substance, can be deadly. What we need to do is to give life the grace of ceremony, not to empty ceremony of life.

Living In Time

8

Living a Future without End

Suppose I had a choice about tomorrow: Either a full and healthy consciousness, or the permanent non-existence of my consciousness. Putting aside other people or practical consequences, which would I choose?

No doubt about it. I'd choose the former.

Yet some of my earlier reasoning led to the conclusion that there's no reason to choose one way rather than the other. If tomorrow I'm conscious, that's fine; but if tomorrow I'm dead, I obviously won't be bothered in the least. Now however, in the light of my more recent reflections, I see that what counts is not the way I will or will not feel in the future. What counts is the impact on me now of my present expectations about that future.

One might suppose that when I made my choice, it was based on the following expectations: choosing one way means I can now look forward to enjoyment, whereas choosing the other way means I can have nothing to look forward to tomorrow. It seems natural to react favorably to the expectation of enjoyment and to choose to have my consciousness continue in existence. Yet here again, as in the case of "separation," the language is confusing.

Strictly speaking, the idiom "I have nothing to look forward to" normally means something like: "I look forward to nothing but misfortune or simply boredom and purposelessness." Or, as one might say, "I'm looking forward to a deadly time"—and that is not at all the same as envisaging the time when I'll be dead. A "deadly time" implies I'm alive and feeling bad. Being dead is *not being*. Why should my future nonexistence be repugnant to me now if I clearly understand that the actual condition will in no way entail having a "deadly time"?

Thus, the key question remains unanswered. What should my present expectation of my death mean to me *subjectively*? It would seem that insofar as it is an expectation of what I will experience, it is an "expectation" that has no content. It certainly is not an expectation of the experience of "nothingness," whatever that would be, for there will be no experience at all. There just is nothing there to expect in my inner world, my lived world, my experience.

How, then, can I compare the inner meaning to me of continued life with the inner meaning to me of death? What is there to compare? "The inner meaning to me of my death" are just words with no content.

One plausible answer is that if "imagining being dead" is in truth not to imagine anything, whereas imagining being alive is imagining pleasures I might have, the latter has a positive attraction. Imagining literally nothing at all neither attracts nor repels. That way of looking at the matter would make the choice of continued existence reasonable, though it would fail to account for positive fear or anguish about ceasing to exist.

Aside from such rather abstract considerations, however, there are more concrete reasons why I have definite desires at present that certain things should be true in the future. Most generally, I have desires about the future even if I don't exist at the time. For example, I would like to think that I have been loyal to the requirements of honest scholarship during my career. I would hate to think that after I died a certain colleague who has had bitter disagreements with me would pursue a pattern of slander in which his false accusations would go unanswered. So I have a stake now in a future that I'll never live to see. Then, too, for example, I have deep desires for the success of certain of my daughter's professional ambitions, ambitions whose outcome I probably will not live to see. Her success or failure will mean nothing to me then. My feelings at that time are of no importance in my present expectations because I know that there will be no feelings at all. Still, my hopes and expectations now are of great importance in my life now.

We do often take into account how we *will* feel about something in the future. Yet what is truly fundamental is how we feel about it now. Maybe I can foresee that I might develop into a more close-minded person as I grow older, and that I would then be perfectly happy indulging in my opinionated pronouncements on controversial issues. Yet that expectation does not make me happy now. I would not now choose that road to happiness. So the fact that in the future when I'm dead there will be no feelings at all does not settle what that prospect means to me now. The failure to realize this has been a source of confusion for me. I have been assuming that my appraisal of what my death means to me depends on what I will feel (or won't feel) at that time. The truth is that the appraisal should depend on how I feel *now* about any particular future, not how I'll feel then.

Now I can see that there are ways in which the future has a meaning for me now that specifically make reasonable my desire to be alive rather then dead. Suppose I look into the distant future and see my little grandson, John, as an adult, mature and in mid-life. Since my grandson is only a five-year-old now, happily slaying dragons, wearing helmet, sword, and shield, I can have only the faintest and most uncertain glimpses of what he will be like as an adult. But I hunger to know—and I know I never will. Yet it makes sense for me to wish now that at that time I'd still be alive to see and be with him. My death means to me now that I will never know his future, never be able to talk and be with him, perhaps help him, have him know me. All such doomed wishes are real elements of the present subjective meaning of my future death. They are a source of legitimate *present* sadness. It's what I want now and expect now that counts, not necessarily how I'll feel or what I'll want—or not feel and not want—in that distant future. It's akin to the way Desdemona's expressions of love in Act I are suffused with our awareness of her eventual death at Othello's hands in the final act.

Perhaps most fundamental of all in understanding what the future means to us and why we want to *be* in the future is the fact that consciousness is in its very nature an active reaching out toward a future. This reaching to the future is not something one can do or not do, want or not want, depending on one's choice. Even when we wish to recall some past event, we are reaching to a future: The recollection *will* be evoked as a result of my present intent to do so. There is no act of consciousness without an aim, that is, without movement toward a future.

Or to make this point the other way around: Without a future, we are "dead to the world." Imagine a state of mind where the future plays no role. There would be, in the idiomatic sense, nothing going on, no business of life, no purposeful moment. Perhaps such a condition exists in the neonate infant, or in the totally apathetic sufferer from advanced Alzheimer's disease. Literally to be without purpose is to lack something essential to the fully human mind.

The prospect of death may be only an inchoate threat, but it is a fundamental threat to this future-oriented aspect of my nature as a conscious being. I say "inchoate threat" not because I lack the strength or intelligence to acknowledge the precise nature of the threat. I can say the words, "This life of mine will end." I can manipulate the logical implications of those words. I can say it, but what I can't get is the *feel* or, more strictly, the *consciousness* of a total absence of a future. To be conscious of no future is in a way a contradiction in terms.

The threat of no future is, from the subjective standpoint, an eerily ungraspable presence. Specific dangers, known and understood, can arouse fear. But the unknown danger—the sound (*was* it a sound?) downstairs in the middle of the night— elicits a strangely penetrating quiver of fright. Hence the special thrill that ghosts and spooks evoke in children, and the terror these things have aroused in credulous adults. So, for a being whose essence is to be moving into a future, the idea of no future is the presence of an invisible ghost, the sound in the dark, the unknowable, intangible, dim apprehension of the unimaginable.

There is a reason why one might think it odd that we can yearn to continue to live. The reason is simply that, generally speaking, I don't yearn for what I know is utterly impossible. I may daydream about such things—the wish to have power to soar at will above the earth, my childhood wish that I'd been born a prince. Yet I never seriously desire such things, never seriously yearn for them, never grieve over their unachievability. Why then do I grieve that I will not follow my grandson's life, or be with my wife, or be able to see the fruition of long term projects to which I've been dedicated? How can I have such strong desires and feelings about these specific things in spite of my knowledge? Here it's not a matter of the general truth that consciousness is future oriented; it's a matter of yearning for specific things that I know without question to be impossible even while I yearn for them. How is this any different from wishing I could have been born a prince, or able to fly like a bird?

Perhaps the answer is that I cannot seriously wish for the impossible things that have never been in the realm of the possible for me. But the things that have been a part of my real life can have a kind of imaginative reality for me. In thinking of myself seeing my grandson as an adult, I am imaginatively constructing a scene made up of familiar kinds of real life situations, real life and familiar people, though I am also aware of the impossibility of this particular scene. The resultant tension between the awareness of the objective impossibility and the subjectively imagined situation with its real life aura produces that unique mixture of yearning and despair which give that future its meaning for me.

In addition to the character of consciousness as inherently pointed toward a future, there is a practical reason, a powerful one, why I am unable to imagine the absence of a future. In the real world, I know that it's possible I may be dead tomorrow. Yet I can't plan and act on that basis, at least so long as I continue in reasonable health. As a practical matter, I have always assumed an indefinite period ahead in which life will continue as usual. I *must* assume this. I must look to tomorrow and tomorrow as days of life, even though I know that at some unspecifiable point there will be no tomorrow. Thinking of ourselves as moving into the future is the rule of everyday practice, of common sense, of long-term habit.

Gabriel García Márquez tells the tale of an old woman who dreams that her time has come. She is a practical woman, and so most of the tale consists in telling the things she does to make ready for her death—the graveyard and burial arrangements, and the elaborate arrangements for her dog. The prospect of death now sets her practical agenda, the future toward which she thinks and acts. In the end, the actual future turns out to be otherwise. She remains alive and well. She had misread the dream. García Márquez's story illustrates that even where death looms as our future, we live *toward* it, so long as we live.

The impulse to look and live toward a future is unquenchable except under the most special conditions. Yet this impulse exists side by side with the objective knowledge that there will come a point where one has no future.

9

Living a Present without Bounds

𝒯he preceding thoughts about the future bring to mind once again the old adage, "live in the moment." How odd that advice is. Taken literally, it's utterly superfluous. As if there were any alternative! But what about the future? It's our nature to live with purpose, to have goals. Shouldn't we be seriously committed to these? It seems a contradiction to say: Be whole-heartedly committed to the goals you set yourself—but live in the moment.

The paradox is resolved when we examine the inward experience of time. The goals I set for myself, and the future as I see it ahead of me, are present to me now. The past, too, insofar as it exists for me, insofar as it registers in my consciousness, is present to me now. In short the future and past as I now inwardly know and experience them are part of my present moment. They are the time-dimensions that give the moment its direction. I understand my present in terms of the past out of which I see it as coming and the future toward which I see it going.

To be specific, what I'm writing at this moment would make no sense to me were I not in some form aware of what I've written up to this point. Even though it's in the background of my consciousness, I must be aware of what I wrote in the previous paragraph if this paragraph and the next ones are to make sense. I also need to have in mind some sense of the idea I'm seeking to put into words, and I have to be conscious of my ultimate goal. How could I proceed now if I had no present consciousness of all this?

Present to me also, though mostly in the background of my consciousness, are the things I've read in the relevant works of others—facts and theories of history, philosophy, science, culture, human nature. All this contributes actively to what I'm doing now. Were not this prior background knowledge active in my consciousness now, my writing would quickly lose direction. I would ignore what past writings and ideas are relevant. I'd make mistakes of fact. My work would lose relevance, become shallow, simply go wrong.

A great deal can be learned from games and sports about the relationship between having goals and "living in the moment." If I'm playing baseball, for example, the goal of winning is part of the future as I *now* envisage it. That goal gives meaning to my present activity. Equally important, my present activity gives meaning to the goal, for the notion of "winning" would lose all sense apart from the game. It's *playing the game* that makes winning meaningful and fulfilling. Only if it is the outcome of the game does "win" or "lose" have any meaning at all. Much the same is true of each element of the game—hitting, running, catching, pitching. There is a distinctive significance that each derives from its role in the game as a whole. One can go through essentially the same bodily motions as in the game— the hit, for example, may be physically the same in the game as it is in practice, but the significance the hit has in the game is markedly different from the significance it has in mere practice.

We can look at life's activities in much the same way. The touchstone questions as to whether one is "living in the moment" are these: Is my fundamental interest the present activity—the game as a whole, the project on the job, the writing of the book? Or is my interest mainly, or wholly, in some hoped-for outcome of the activity—to win, to earn money, to receive the rewards of success? In the latter cases, the activity itself is mere labor, of value only as a means to my goal. The time spent is life expended, surrendered, without any value of its own to me.

Living in the present, then, does not mean rejecting interest in future outcomes. It is a rejection of a certain *kind* of interest—an interest solely in an isolated part of the present (the envisaged goal) rather than in the whole of the present activity.

This distinction is crucial in the doctrine that is so fundamental to Hindu and Buddhist thought, the doctrine of *karma* ("action"). That doctrine teaches that we should not be "attached" to the "fruits" of "action.—The concept of "action" here connotes a coherent project, a course of conduct that is engaged in purposefully. To be unattached to the fruits of action does not mean we should act without interest in the goals and rewards to be achieved. It means to be committed to the present action *as a whole*. The Bhagavad Gita teaches that this necessarily includes commitment to goals in their role as essential elements of the action. But commitment to the goal as the sole or fundamental thing of value is confusion.

This teaching is akin to the idea I discussed earlier: Human consciousness is inherently future-oriented. The Gita acknowledges this. Consciousness is equally oriented to a past and to the present. To devalue any of these is a confusion of values. The doctrine of *karma* is directed squarely to this idea: We must live for the whole of the moment, not just for the hoped-for results, not just with nostalgia for a past, not just with near-sighted concern for a present in which past and future are ignored.

There's nothing esoteric about this. I know from experience what a difference it makes whether I love the game (including the element of striving to win), or whether I love primarily to be the victor, the game itself being merely a necessary labor if I'm to have a chance to win. In this latter case the game becomes an exercise in ego, and the threat of losing becomes a threat to my ego. However, when it's playing the game that interests me, I enjoy playing the game—win *or* lose. Of course, I try as hard as I can to win. Trying to win is an essential part of wholeheartedly playing the game. Yet if I do lose, I can still honestly say I enjoyed the game and it was worth playing. There's all the difference between aiming to win as part of playing the game, and aiming to win in order to satisfy one's ego.

As we approach that horizon we call death, the prospect of expending the remaining stretches of our life in sterile fashion ought to cause increasing dismay. After all, success in any venture and enjoyment of its fruits are a chancy matter. If the fruits were all that counted, then failure means the effort was totally wasted, part of one's life spent for nothing. Then, too, I've found that many things I had hoped for with great anticipation turned out to be ashes in my mouth. The toy I longed for as a child, the car I saved for, the higher rank I expected so much from, the honor to be awarded—all turned out to be pleasures adulterated by conflicting elements, pleasures disappointingly transient. I've seen so many young professors who find they don't enjoy the research-publication called for in the University, but who carry on with the burden in order to hold the job, then in order to get a promotion, then to get tenure, and so on, always pressing to the next goal. Each goal is promising in the expectation, so transiently satisfying in the achievement. At every step the brief satisfaction of achieving the goal is followed promptly by the oppressive realization that still another goal, calling for arduous and unsatisfying labor, looms ahead. The pattern is inevitable for one who is "attached to the fruits of action" and does not realize that this is a confusion of values. Looked at objectively, most of a professional life lived in that way is meaningless drudgery, accompanied by chronic tension, and is so in spite of any social status or material comforts achieved.

On the other hand, if the activity itself is fulfilling, any ultimate lack of success is at most a negative moment in a satisfying life, not final evidence of the futility of life. In fact, for a life well-lived, the risk of failure adds spice to the enterprise in the way that the risk of losing a well-played game makes the game itself so exciting.

These reflections about the primacy of the activity help me to understand a familiar but puzzling phenomenon in the course of many years of writing. After putting much time, effort, and enthusiasm into writing an article or a book, I find that when it's completed the interest I had in the work disappears. Of course, I hope it will be a work of value to its audience. But I have noticed often that my own personal interest in it disappears.

I think this is not a unique reaction. I have the impression that it's common among writers and creative workers generally. The creative interest lies in the activity—the act of creation. Once the work has come to fruition, the perspective of the activity of creation is gone, and the work loses the significance it had in that perspective. It no longer represents a work *being* created; it is a work that *was* created but that now stands on its own, independent of the creative act.

The finished work may in turn become a source of other kinds of personal gratifications for the creator, especially if the work meets with success. The work may arouse public interest and lively comment. Money, status, or other benefits may accrue and be enjoyed. The work may be one in a projected series and from that perspective retain interest for the creator.

Still, in a very important way, the creative artist is liberated from the work when it is done. It is the doing that's of central value, and the finished work has value to the artist in much the same way that a well deserved win in a sport has value. It is in its status as culmination of an activity that the win or the art object has significance to the player or the creator.

This whole question of living in the moment can also be understood from a very different standpoint. Earlier I spoke of myself as an inhabitant of the world, located at a certain point in time and space, interacting with other inhabitants of my time. In short, I am *in* the world. Then I contrasted this with the other subjective perspective: The world is in me. That is, *all* of this world—past, present, and future—is present to my consciousness, contained within my consciousness. Putting things into this double perspective can help illuminate what is meant by living in the moment.

My role as inhabitant of the world emphasizes the more familiar viewpoint from which the past is seen as gone, and the future as not yet. Only the present is "real." I can, however, adopt the other perspective: I am the center of the world, the consciousness of the whole. The past of my inner world, as I know it, is the past that is present to this consciousness. The future I foresee for this inner world of mine is the future as it is present to me now. Or, to put it slightly differently, the past and the future, so far as they exist in my world, are dimensions of this actual present moment which I am living. All this is easy to illustrate.

In the midst of reading a mystery story, I am located at a point somewhere within the story, with a past defined by the opening crime and a future defined by the goal of discovering the identity of the guilty party. I tend to take the standpoint of the detective, the inhabitant of the story world, a person focused on achieving his overarching aim—solution of the crime. This is a necessary point of view if I'm to enter properly into the story. Identifying with the detective as an inhabitant of the (novel's) world, I am inclined to think that the solution of the crime is the central value. However, the larger truth is that the central value of the story—if it's well written—lies not in the solution to the crime but in the activity of reading. The value lies in the suspenseful enjoyment of each moment. Each present moment is enjoyed because it contains awareness of the past—the crime—and all that has happened since, as well as awareness of the sought for future—the solution of the crime. In that context I appreciate what is currently happening in the present time of the story. Past and future are dimensions of the present, dimensions *within* the present. The aim of solving the crime is no more than an element that contributes to the pleasurable suspense of my present reading. If I'm clearly aware of this, I see that what I really want is for the story to go on, not to get to the goal as quickly as possible. I have to be genuinely interested in achieving the goal, but attachment to the fruits—the solution of the crime *for its own sake*—makes no sense.

So, from the standpoint of this way of looking at consciousness, I can see again that it is indeed confusion, as the Gita says, to place all my hopes on the future fruits of my actions. It is blindness to discount the equally real—or perhaps even more real—present and past.

If I wait for my fulfillment in some dreamed-of future success, if I live attached to that dream, then it's desperately necessary that I flee Death lest he come before the dream comes true. Otherwise I have lost all. I would have to keep running from this present, interested only in that dream-city of Samara, not knowing that Samara is the place of my rendezvous with Death.

Perspective on Life and Death

10

"Before, I had heard—
Now I see"

$\mathcal{N}$ow I see the whole picture in a new light. There is a conception implicit in much that I've said. It has finally come to me with clarity. I can get at it best by recalling that again and again I've run into paradoxes.

I've remarked, for example, on the obvious truth that when my life is viewed from the standpoint of all time, space, and existence, it appears as a momentary flicker that in the next moment is snuffed out. I came out of and disappear into the infinite anonymity of space and time. From this perspective I can't escape a sense of the profound insignificance of this life of mine. What was paradoxical was the undeniable fact that my life is of momentous significance to me. The world is the content of my consciousness. I am the center, the audience for the show. My death is the end of the world, the only world I know. As a speck in the cosmos, how can I take this life seriously? On the other hand, as the only life I have, how can I *not* take it seriously? The prospect of death can make precious each moment, no matter how trivial; but on the other hand the prospect of death can make even things of importance seem trivial.

Another paradox: I know for a certainty I will die—but I know for an equal certainty that I will never live to see this happen. Still another: I spoke of seeing myself as one particular inhabitant and actor *in* the world, and yet also as the unique consciousness that contains all the world within it. I also said that subjectively the idea of death as the end of consciousness is the idea of nothing, or rather an idea with no conscious content, a blank. Yet I have had to try to puzzle out why so many powerful emotions are evoked by an idea with no content.

Throughout this exploration I've continually run up against the phenomenon of differing perspectives that generate contradictory or at least paradoxical perceptions of the meaning of life and of death. My aim has been to find which one is the correct perspective. Or at least I have wanted to find some perspective that is reasonable enough for me to adopt as my fundamental one. I had hoped to find a perspective that would enable me to confront death with equanimity rather than terror and anguish. My constant and fundamental question has been: *In the last analysis*, how am I to look at my life and death?

I see now that the answer has been there all along, unrecognized because the question was wrongly framed. I was presuming that there exists one ultimate perspective on death that is the correct perspective, or at least the one most to be preferred. My presupposition was that there could be a "last analysis," a final answer.

Can there be such an ultimate perspective? Since the word "perspective" as I use it here is obviously a metaphor derived from its literal use in connection with vision, it will help to recall how perspectives work in vision.

There's a stunning skyscraper (one of many) we saw on a recent visit to Toronto. We noticed it first while standing on the sidewalk a few blocks away. It was an enormous, yet razor thin and seamless shape gleaming in the sun, soaring into the sky. We later looked for it from our eighth story hotel window on a different street. We had difficulty identifying it; the perspective was so different. Then we did see it—it was a striking, jaggedly step-wise shape, neither razor thin nor seamless. Still later, from the top of the CN Tower (itself the tallest structure in the world), we looked down on the city's skyscrapers and could hardly identify the building we sought. When we did, we saw it as flat, gray, and unimposing among all the other striking sky-scrapers that fill the Toronto skyline.

Which is the way it *really* looks? Which was the *correct* perspective?

The answer is obvious. There are as many correct perceptions of that building as there are perspectives from which to view it. Each "look" was authentic, a fact about the world. Each perspective presents a specific and correct view of the building. What was a matter of choice, indeed the crucial choice, was the choice of perspective. The "look" from that perspective was a given, not a choice.

Human beings have a tendency—at least I know I have it—to try to avoid multiple perspectives. We want to see things in one simple, familiar way, to settle on one right perspective, revealing how a thing "really" looks, what a thing "really" is. We do not want complexity, ambiguity, or apparent contradiction. This tendency to seek one all-sufficing perspective was reflected in my own former search for the "correct" perspective on my own mortality.

I now see still another reason why there is such universal appeal in games, sports, drama, literature. They all provide an unambiguous basic perspective. They define a beginning, a middle, and an end. The Narrator consciousness, or a game-defined perspective, is *the* overarching perspective to which all else is subordinate. This unambiguity is a release from the tension of multiple perspectives in everyday life.

It's notable, however, that a device used in art and literature to increase interest is to build several different perspectives into the work—the plane surface of the painting in tension with the three-dimensional depth depicted, the shift in the novel from one character's point of view to that of others. This builds tension, suspense, uncertainty. But even so, there is an unambiguous ultimate perspective—the frame of the painting, the beginning and end of the novel. Just as the suspense and changing fortunes in a competitive game generate both tension and increased intensity of pleasure, so do multiple perspectives on life and death increase tension, while also enriching our life.

Nevertheless, the temptation is to avoid the tensions. Religious doctrines have ubiquitous attraction in good part because, like games and works of art, they define one ultimate perspective. They provide *the* answer. Tension and ambiguity are dispelled. Moreover, the appeal of that single perspective is vastly enhanced when religious doctrines place the fate of human beings at the center of the theological drama. And these doctrines acquire still further attractiveness when that ultimate perspective on existence portrays a world ruled by justice and love.

Real life, on the other hand, is messy. It frequently offers no single "right" perspective. We find it difficult to figure out how to take the situation, difficult to decide which is the best perspective on the matter at hand. I think of a rather trivial example which represents the everydayness of what I mean. I gave my grandson a much wanted computer game. From one perspective I saw this gift as a genuinely generous and loving one. And I believe it truly was such. From another angle I nevertheless had to ask myself, Am I spoiling him? Will his parents think I'm spoiling him? From still another perspective I asked myself, Am I indulging my need to be loved? I had to acknowledge there was something to that. Then, too, the question arose whether in providing him with still another computer game would I contribute to decreasing his interest in books and reading? There were these and still other questions, from so many perspectives, even in so minor a matter as this.

It's not only that the perspectives are multiple, and therefore the look of a situation can be so changing. What's particularly troubling is that the different "looks" often clash with one another. One feels they can't both be "true," or both be "right," or even both be reasonable. Often the dilemma we face in life is not which action to take but the perplexing decision as to which perspective to take. Once the problem of adopting a perspective is resolved, the appropriate course of action is frequently obvious. Of course, ignorance of the facts can also be a problem. Yet often when we do know the facts, this still doesn't resolve our dilemma. For example, we may know there will be an increase in the national debt if we double the subsidies for college education, and we also may believe that this will result in a certain improved level of education. The crucial choice is whether we are to look at the matter from the perspective of budgetary impact, or from the perspective of the human and social impact.

The same is true of the complexities of personal relationships. In these truly important matters, as well as in matters of social policy, we rarely have *all* the relevant facts. Indeed, whether a fact is relevant at all depends on the perspective one takes. For example, I never sought the facts about the level of difficulty of the computer game I gave my elder grandson. Facts of that kind were irrelevant. Why? Because, knowing my grandson's skills with the computer, I had no need to examine the game from that perspective.

In complex matters, we often do at the outset what we would have to do anyway even after deep inquiry. The facts in such cases rarely suffice to settle the matter. Instead, we settle matters in the light of the general perspectives we favor, be they those of the conservative, the liberal, the devout, the atheist, the environmentalist, the moralist, or whatever. Hence we see the persistent differences of opinion—moral, religious, political, ideological—that defy the conciliatory powers of "sweet Reason." The initial perspective predetermines the general nature of the ultimate judgment by each party on each issue.

Although the choice among multiple perspectives is often a troubling task, the capacity to view life from multiple perspectives is also a wonderfully distinctive feature of human nature. It is this capacity that distinguishes us from animals. To be human is to be able to consider things from alternate points of view. The meaning to me of my existence is enriched and deepened as I view my life from more and more perspectives. These may engender conflicting visions, but that adds to the excitement and richness of life.

I see now that what I wanted in exploring the meaning of my death was to be able to face reality—comfortably. Well, certain perspectives do provide much comfort. Others, however, provide little or none.

And I see now that I have to live with the necessity to view my life and death from many equally valid perspectives, often radically clashing. These include the perspectives on life and death that have emerged and clashed in the course of these chapters.

Can one live on the basis of multiple visions?

The answer is: One must.

Will they form a harmonious whole?

Of course not.

This peculiarly human dilemma lends inescapable irony, tragedy, and comedy to the human drama. Yet, in the end, we have no reasonable option. The alternative is to adopt a blind adherence to some single perspective, and thus live the impoverished life of the dogmatist or the fanatic.

The Book of Job is a source of insight for me in this connection. It vividly reveals the role that multiple perspectives must have in understanding our existence. Many people mistakenly read that work as teaching that God is a mystery, and we simply have to accept on faith that the world is ultimately good and just and rational. Job, an honest man, was compelled to cry out that the undeniable evidence of his own fate refuted this view. That is the point of his lengthy complaints. He claims he has acted justly (and we have the Lord's word for the truth of this in the Introduction). Yet Job in his misery claims (quite correctly) that he is being meted out an unjust fate. It was not that Job's complaint was factually wrong. The truth that was finally revealed to Job was that his complaint from the single perspective of justice was laughably inadequate.

The Voice out of the tempest ridicules Job's belief that justice ought to prevail in this world. In place of this simple-minded, impoverished view of Existence, the Voice reveals a cosmos of dazzling complexity, a cosmos that embodies the terrifying and the glorious, the tame and the savage, justice and injustice, the creative and the destructive, heavenly harmonies and chaos. The Voice reveals a cosmos of unimaginable variety, a cosmos that can't be described or understood from any one perspective. It is a cosmos of enormous energy and infinitely many attributes, to be viewed from incomprehensibly many perspectives. In this lies its magnificence, and our human potential for appreciating such magnificence makes us "like unto the angels."

In the eyes of the Lord, Job's presumption that the cosmos was understandable from a single perspective, though the orthodox perspective of the time, amounted to trivializing the awesome and dazzling infinity of Existence. When, at last, the Lord has revealed all this, Job is profoundly humbled. Before, he had only heard what others said. "Now, I see." His ego, with its misguided pride in his virtue, "melts away." While this selflessness is humbling, the revelation is enriching and liberating. Thus, paradoxically, Job achieves a new and greater dignity, a far richer spirituality. In the folk-tale metaphor of the story's conclusion, he ends up a far richer man than ever before.

To bear the tension of seeing life from many different perspectives is not quite so improbable a feat as it may seem. There are routine and tensionless times precisely because there are situations where the perspectives happen to harmonize, or at least don't clash. But we cannot honestly evade the fact that on occasion they do clash and lead to conflict among the alternatives we face. And we do live with this dilemma. My prior reflections suggest to me that the confrontation with death is the test *par excellence* of one's will and ability to live with multiple perspectives.

I had hoped for easier answers in thinking about my death. Instead I've found unsettling truth, the truth that life and death have many truths. The question is whether I can live, and die, by that unsettling truth.

PART TWO

OTHER VOICES, OTHER VISIONS

Introduction

$\mathcal{A}$s the reader will recognize, this second part of the book follows the first in logical sequence. It can also stand by itself as an introduction to the reflections of some of the greatest minds on the meaning of death.

The texts that follow are extracts from larger works, philosophical in character. The selecting, editing, and abridging are my responsibility. My aim has been to present material from different times and places that bears directly on matters raised in part 1. Needless to say, the collection that follows is neither "complete" nor representative of all points of view.

I have, however, grouped the selections. I believe that reading each selection in conjunction with others in the same group, and the groups in contrast to each other, can reveal a certain provocative relevance.

In editing and in translating these selections I have tried to make sure that each brief text is coherent and readable by a reader unfamiliar with the original full text. I should stress, however, that in all cases of these kinds, the translation and editing result in a text whose content and tone remain consistent with extant authoritative translations.

Section 1

Leo Tolstoy

Blaise Pascal

Miguel de Unamuno

Leo Tolstoy

Leo Tolstoy, 1828–1910, Russia. After having written such masterpieces as War and Peace *and* Anna Karenina, *Tolstoy went through a spiritual crisis and became a passionate convert to a version of Christianity emphasizing love, pacifism, and poverty. In addition to various nonfictional works expounding these views, he wrote the short masterpiece of fiction, "The Death of Ivan Ilyich."*

The following selection consists of extracts from his essay, "My Confession," in which he narrates the course of his spiritual development, and in particular the spiritual crisis that led him from a rationalistic, humanistic outlook to that of a devout Christian.

I was christened and educated in the Orthodox Christian Faith; I was taught it in my childhood, and in my boyhood and youth. Nevertheless, when, at eighteen years of age, I left the university in the second year, I had discarded all belief in anything I had been taught.

To judge by what I can now remember, I never had a serious belief; I merely trusted in what my elders made their profession of faith, but even this trust was very precarious.

This estrangement from all belief went on in me, as it does

now, and always has done, in those of the same social position and culture. This falling off, as it seems to me, for the most part goes on thus: people live as others live, and their lives are guided, not by the principles of the faith that is taught them, but by their very opposite. Belief has no influence on life, nor on the relations among men—it is relegated to some other sphere apart from life and independent of it. If the two ever come into contact at all, belief is only one of the outward phenomena, and not one of the constituent parts of life.

In my writings I taught what for me was the only truth— that the object of life should be our highest happiness and that of our family.

Thus I lived; but, five years ago, a strange state of mind began to grow upon me: I had moments of perplexity, of a stoppage, as it were, of life, as if I did not know how I was to live, what I was to do, and I began to wander, and was a victim to low spirits. But this passed, and I continued to live as before. Later, these periods of perplexity began to return more and more frequently, and invariably took the same form. These stoppages of life always presented themselves to me with the same questions: "Why?" and "What after?"

At first it seemed to me that these were aimless, unmeaning questions. It seemed to me that all they asked about was well known, and that if at any time when I wished to find answers to them I could do so without much trouble—that just at that time I could not be bothered with this, but whenever I should stop to think them over I should find an answer. But these questions presented themselves to my mind with ever increasing frequency, demanding an answer with still greater and greater persistence, and like dots grouped themselves into one black spot.

It was with me as it happens in the case of every mortal internal ailment—at first appear the insignificant symptoms of indisposition, disregarded by the patient; then these symptoms are repeated more and more frequently, till they merge in uninterrupted suffering. The sufferings increase, and the patient, before he has time to look around, is confronted with the fact that what he took for a mere indisposition has become more important to him than anything else on earth, that it is death!

This is exactly what happened to me. I became aware that this was not a chance indisposition, but something very serious, and that if all these questions continued to recur, I should have to find an answer to them. And I tried to answer them. The questions seemed so foolish, so simple, so childish; but no sooner had I taken hold of them and attempted to decide them than I was convinced, first, that they were neither childish nor silly, but were concerned with the deepest problems of life; and, in the second place, that no matter how I put my mind upon them I could not answer them.

Before occupying myself with my Samara estate, with the education of my son, with the writing of books, I was bound to know why I did these things. As long as I do not know the reason "why" I cannot do anything, I cannot live. While thinking about the management of my household and estate, which in these days occupied much of my time, suddenly this question came into my head:—

"Well and good, I have now six thousand desyatins of land in Samara, and three hundred horses—what then?"

I was thoroughly disconcerted, and knew not what to think. Another time, dwelling on the thought of how I should educate my children, I asked myself, "What for?" Again, when considering by what means the well-being of the people might best be promoted, I suddenly exclaimed, "But what concern have I with it?" When I thought of the fame which my works were gaining me, I said to myself—"Well, what if I should be more famous than Gogol, Pushkin, Shakespear, Molière—than all the writers of the world—well, and what then?" I could find no reply. Such questions will not wait. They demand an immediate answer and without one it is impossible to live. But answer there was none.

I felt that the ground on which I stood was crumbling, that there was nothing for me to stand on, that what I had been living for was nothing, that I had no reason for living.

My life had come to a stop. I was able to breathe, to eat, to drink, to sleep, and I could not help breathing, eating, drinking, sleeping; but there was no real life in me because I had not a single desire, the fulfilment of which I could feel to be reasonable. If I wished for anything, I knew beforehand that, were I to satisfy the wish, or were I not to satisfy it, nothing would come of it. Had a fairy appeared and offered me all I desired, I should not have known what to say. If I had, in moments of excitement, what were not wishes but the habits of former wishes, at calmer moments I knew that it was a delusion, that I really wished for nothing. I could not even wish to know the truth, because I guessed in what it consisted.

The truth was, that life was meaningless. Every day of life, every step in it, brought me, as it were, nearer the precipice, and I saw clearly that before me there was nothing but ruin. And to stop was impossible; to go back was impossible; and it was impossible to shut my eyes so as not to see that there was nothing before me but suffering and actual death, absolute annihilation.

Thus I, a healthy and a happy man, was brought to feel that I could live no longer,—some irresistible force was dragging me onward to escape from life. I do not mean that I wished to kill myself.

The force that drew me away from life was stronger, fuller, and more universal than any wish, it was a force like that of my previous attachment to life, only in a contrary direction. All my strength impelled me away from life. The idea of suicide came as naturally to me as formerly that of bettering my life. This thought was so attractive to me that I was compelled to practise upon myself a species of self-deception in order to avoid carrying it out too hastily. I was unwilling to act hastily, only because I wanted to employ all my powers in clearing away the confusion of my thoughts; if I should not clear them away, I could at any time kill myself. And here was I, a man fortunately situated, hiding away a cord, to avoid being tempted to hang myself by it to the transom between the closets of my room, where I undressed alone every evening. And I ceased to go hunting with a gun because it offered too easy a way of getting rid of life. I myself did not know what I wanted; I was afraid of life; I struggled to get away from it, and yet there was something I hoped for *from* it.

Such was the condition I had come to, at a time when all the circumstances of my life were preeminently happy ones, and when I had not reached my fiftieth year. I had a good, loving, and beloved wife, good children, and a large estate, which, without much trouble on my part, was growing and increasing; I was more than ever respected by my friends and acquaintances; I was praised by strangers, and could lay claim to having made my name famous without much self-deception. Moreover, I was not mad or in an unhealthy mental state; on the contrary, I enjoyed a mental and physical strength which I have seldom found in men of my class and pursuits; I could keep up with a peasant in mowing, and could continue mental labor for eight or ten hours at a stretch, without any evil consequences. And in this state of things it came to this,—that I could not live, and as I feared death I was obliged to employ ruses against myself so as not to put an end to my life.

It was this that was terrible! And to get free from this horror, I was ready to kill myself. I felt a horror of what awaited me; I knew that this horror was more horrible than the position I was in itself, but I could not patiently await the end.

In my search for a solution of the problem of life, I experienced the same feeling as a man who is lost in a forest. He comes to an open plain, climbs up a tree, and sees clearly around him a space without end, but nowhere his home—nor could it be there. He goes into the thick of the wood, into the darkness, and sees darkness, but again no home.

Thus had I lost my way in the forest of human knowledge, in the light of the mathematical and experimental sciences which opened out for me clear horizons where there could be no home, and in the darkness of philosophy, plunging me into a greater gloom with every step I took, until I was at last persuaded that there was, and could be, no way out.

Having failed to find an explanation in knowledge, I began to seek it in life itself, hoping to find it in the men who surrounded me; and I began to watch men like myself, to observe how they lived, and how they in their practice treated the question that had brought me to despair.

And this is what I found among those of the same social position and culture as myself:

I found that for the people of my class there were four means of escape from the terrible state in which we all were.

The first means of escape is through ignorance. It consists in not perceiving and understanding that life is an evil and an absurdity. People of this class—for the greater part women, or very young or very stupid men—have not understood the problem of life as it presented itself to Schopenhauer, to Solomon, and to Buddha. They see neither the dragon awaiting them, nor the mice eating through the plant to which they cling, and they lick the drops of honey. But they only lick the honey for a time—something directs their attention to the dragon and the mice, and then there is an end to their licking. From these I could learn nothing: we cannot unknow what we do know.

The second means of escape is the Epicurean. It consists, even while we know the hopelessness of taking advantage of every good there is in life, in avoiding the sight of the dragon and mice, and in the meantime in seeking the honey as best we can, especially wherever there is most of it. Solomon points out this issue from the difficulty thus:—

"Then I commended mirth, because a man hath no better thing under the sun, than to eat, and to drink, and to be merry: for that shall abide with him of his labor the days of his life, which God giveth him under the sun.... Go thy way, eat thy bread with joy, and drink thy wine with a merry heart.... Live joyfully with the wife whom thou lovest all the days of the life of thy vanity, which he hath given thee under the sun, all the days of thy vanity: for that is thy portion in this life, and in thy labor which thou takest under the sun. Whatsoever thy hand findeth to do, do it with thy might; for there is no work, nor device, nor knowledge, nor wisdom, in the grave, whither thou goest."

It is thus that most of the people of our circle maintain the possibility of living. The conditions in which they are placed cause them to know more of the good than the evil of life, and their moral obtuseness enables them to forget that all the advantages of their position are accidental, and that not all men can have harems and palaces, like Solomon; that for one man who has a thousand wives, there are a thousand men who have none, and for each palace there must be thousands of men to build it in the sweat of their brow, and that the same chance which has made me a Solomon to-day may make me Solomon's slave tomorrow. The dullness of their imagination enables these men to forget what destroyed the peace of Buddha, the inevitable sickness, old age, and death, which if not to-day, then to-morrow, must be the end of all their pleasures.

Thus think and feel the majority of the men of our time and class. That some of them call their dullness of thought and imagination by the name of positive philosophy, does not in my opinion separate them from those who, in order not to see the real question, lick the honey. I could not imitate such as these; not having their obtuseness of imagination, I could not artificially prevent its action. Like every man who really lives, I could not turn my eyes aside from the mice and the dragon, when I had once seen them.

The third means of escape is through strength and energy. It consists in destroying life when we have perceived that it is an evil and an absurdity. Only the rare men, strong and logical, act thus. Understanding all the stupidity of the joke that is played on us, and understanding that the happiness of the dead is more than the happiness of the living, and that it is better not to be, they thus act and put an end at once to the stupid Joke, using any means of doing it—a rope round the neck, water, a knife in the heart, or a railway train. The number of those in my own class acting thus continually increases, and those that do this are for the most part in the very prime of life, with their intellectual powers in their flower, and with but few of the habits that undermine man's reason as yet formed.

I saw that this means of escape was the worthiest, and wished to make use of it.

The fourth means of escape is through weakness. It consists, though the evil and absurdity of life are well known, in continuing to drag it out, though aware that nothing can come of it. People of this class know that death is better than life, but have not the strength of character to act as their reason dictates, to have done with deceit and kill themselves; they seem to be waiting for something to happen. This way of escape is due solely to weakness, for if I know what is better, and it is within my reach, why not seize it?. . . To this class of men I myself belonged.

Thus do people of my own class, in four different ways, save themselves from a terrible contradiction. However earnestly I strained my reasoning faculties I could not find any other than these four ways.

I long lived in this state of mental aberration, which, though not always openly expressed in words, is not the less common among the most learned and most liberal men. But whether, owing to my strange kind of instinctive affection for the laboring classes, which impelled me to understand them, and to see that they are not so stupid as we think, or owing to the sincerity of my conviction that I could know nothing beyond the advisability of hanging myself, I felt that, if I wished to live and understand the meaning of life, I must seek it not amongst those who have lost the meaning of life, and wish to kill themselves, but amongst the millions of the living and the dead who have made our life what it is, and on whom now rests the burden of our life and their own.

So I watched the life common to such enormous numbers of the dead and the living, the life of simple, unlearned, and poor men, and found something quite different. I saw that, with rare exceptions, all these millions, who are alive and have lived, did not fit into my classification; I could not count them among those who do not understand the question, because they not only put it, but answer it, with extraordinary clearness. I could not call them Epicureans, because their life has far more of privation and suffering than of enjoyment. To count them amongst those who, against their reason, live through a life without meaning, was still less possible, because every act of their lives, and death itself, is explained by them. Self-murder they regard as the greatest of crimes. It appeared that throughout mankind there is a knowledge of the meaning of life which I had neglected and despised. It resulted, that the knowledge based on reason denies a meaning to life, and excludes life; while the meaning given to life by the millions that form the great whole of humanity is founded on a despised and fallacious knowledge.

The knowledge based on reason, the knowledge of the learned and the wise, denies a meaning in life, while the great mass of men, all humanity, have an unreasoning knowledge of life which gives a meaning to it.

This unreasoning knowledge is the faith which I could not but reject. This is God, one and yet three; this is the creation in six days, devils and angels,—and all that I cannot accept while I keep my senses!

My position was terrible. I knew that from the knowledge which reason has given man; I could get nothing but the denial of life, and from faith nothing but the denial of reason, which last was even more impossible than the denial of life. By the knowledge founded on reason it was proved that life is an evil and that men know it to be so, that men may cease to live if they will, but that they have lived and they go on living—I myself lived on, though I had long known that life was meaningless and evil. If I went by faith it resulted that, in order to understand the meaning of life, I should have to abandon reason, the very part of me that required a meaning in life!

Blaise Pascal

Blaise Pascal, 1623–1662, France. Pascal was a brilliant mathematician and physicist. He made fundamental contributions to each of these disciplines. He underwent a deep religious experience while at the famous convent of Port Royal. His religious leanings were of the Jansenist school, a theology that postulated a mysterious God, and salvation of only the elect by His grace. His posthumously published Reflections (Pensées), *from which the following selection is taken, has become one of the classics of the Western philosophical literature on the meaning and destiny of human life. The translation is mine.*

It takes no very sensitive soul to realize that in this life there is no true and solid satisfaction. Our pleasures are no more than vanity, our troubles unending. In the end death, which threatens at every instant, will inevitably bring us to a terrible fate, either an eternity of suffering, or eternal nothingness.

Nothing is more real, nothing more terrible than this prospect Whatever the show of bravery, such is the end of even the best of lives, however fair the life, such is our end. Think well on it—can you doubt that there is good in this life only if there is the hope of another one, and happiness only in the degree that one nears it. Only those who attest an utter confi-

dence in eternal life are free of misery; while those who do not
see the light know no happiness at all.

Most assuredly it is a great ill to live in such doubt. But then
it is at very least a necessary duty to seek the light. One who
doubts but does not seek is both unhappy, and also morally
wrong. I can find no words to describe such people, particularly
if they are at ease and satisfied, if they proclaim their doubt and
boast of it, and even treat it as a source of pleasure and a reason
for pride.

How can anyone arrive at such feelings? What joy can a person find in expecting nothing but misery without recourse?
What point of pride is there in seeing oneself engulfed in
impenetrable obscurity? How could a rational being reason
along such lines as this, for example:

> "I do not know who put me into this world, nor do I understand what
> the world is, or even what I myself am. My ignorance of all things is
> vast. I do not know the nature of my body, nor of my senses. I do not
> know the nature of my soul, nor do I know the nature of that part of
> me which thinks the thoughts I speak, which contemplates the world,
> and itself as well."

> "I see the awesome empty spaces of the universe; they surround me. I
> myself occupy a tiny corner of this vast extent. I do not know why I
> have been placed in this spot rather than some other, why I have been
> assigned this time in which to live rather than any other moment of
> the eternity that preceded me, or of that which will follow. I see noth-
> ing but infinities surrounding me in every dimension, I, an atom, a
> shadow, lasting a moment only, never to return. All that I know
> speaks of the death I must soon meet, but I pay no attention to this
> death I cannot evade."

> "Just as I do not know from whence I came, so too I do not know
> whither I go. I only know that when I depart this world I will have fall-
> en for evermore either into nothingness or else into the hands of an
> angry God, but I do not know which of the two conditions will be my
> lot. Such is my state, full of weakness and uncertainty."

> "And from all this I deduce that I should pass the days of my life giv-
> ing no thought to what will become of me. Perhaps from within my
> doubts themselves clarity will come. But I lack any desire to take the
> trouble, or even to make the slightest move toward seeking clarity.
> Later on, scorning those who labor at that task,I propose to go with-

out fear or forethought, take on the great event and let myself be led easily to my death, still uncertain of my condition in the eternal future."

Who would wish to have as friend a person who speaks in this way? Who would choose such a person as confidante in life's affairs? Who would turn for help, when afflicted, to that person? Indeed, of what use in life is such a person?

Miguel de Unamuno

Miguel de Unamuno, 1864–1936, Spain. Of Basque origin, he was a writer of novels and poems, and was characterized as the greatest literary figure of Spain in his time. He was also a profound influence on the Spanish philosophical thought of his era. His views on life and death are, characteristically, expressed with passion in his famous work, The Tragic Sense of Life. *The following passages are extracted from that work, and almost entirely from the chapter entitled "The Hunger for Immortality." The translation is mine.*

. . . we remain with the pressing suspicion that the emotional basis of all knowledge is the yearning not to die, the hunger for personal immortality, the drive toward indefinitely continuing our own being. This yearning is the personal, inward point of departure for anyone who would fashion for humankind a humane philosophy. . . . It is this personal and emotional point of departure for all philosophy, and for all religion, that constitutes the tragic sense of life. Let us examine it.

To conceive ourselves as non-existent we need to make some adequate effort of consciousness to become aware of absolute unconsciousness, and thus its own annihilation. Make the effort, Reader: While you are fully awake imagine the state of your soul in deepest sleep . . . . You will see. The attempt at understanding results in the most grievous vertigo. We cannot conceive ourselves as not existing.

Love, and the vanity of this world and its ways—these are the two root tones, the key notes of true poetry. Neither one can sound, but the other must resound as well. The sense of this vanity of the passing world kindles love within us, unique in that it vanquishes what is vain and transitory, unique in that it makes life full and eternalizes it. At least so it appears. . . .

Everything passes! That is the refrain sung by those who have drunk, mouth to the stream of the fountain of life, the refrain of those who have relished the fruit of the tree of knowledge of good and evil.

To be, to be forever, to be without end! The thirst for being, the thirst for more being! . . .

"Ye shall be as gods!," so Genesis tells us the serpent said to the first pair of lovers . . . and all religion derives historically from the cult of the dead—which is to say, of immortality.

The thought that I must die, and the enigma of what will be afterwards—this is the very heartbeat of my consciousness. Contemplating the serenity of the green fields, or contemplating eyes of such clarity that there appears in them the soul of one who is my sister, my consciousness swells, I feel the diastole of the soul and am drenched in the life about me, and I believe in my future. But at just this point the voice of the mystery whispers to me: "Thou wilt cease to be!" The Angel of Death brushes me with his wing, and in the systole of the soul the depths of my spirit are inundated by the blood of divinity.

Like Pascal, I do not understand someone who claims not to care a whit about this matter. This carelessness in a matter that "concerns themselves, their eternal; fate, and their all, is something that irritates me more than it evokes my compassion; it amazes me and horrifies me." One who feels thus "is for me (as for Pascal, whose words I have been quoting) a monster."

When nothing more than mud shacks and thatch huts were built for the living, to disintegrate under the ravages of the weather, tumuli were erected for the dead; and before ever stone was used for habitation, it was used for sepulchres. The houses of the dead have been strong enough to stand against the centuries, but not the houses of the living, not the inns of passage, but the abodes that endure.

Sickness? Perhaps. But who does not take care for sickness neglects health; the human animal is in essence and in substance sick. Sickness? Perhaps this is so because life itself is prisoner, and the only health possible is death. Yet this sickness is the fountain from which true health flows. From the depths of this anguish, from the abyss of our sense of mortality, we come out into the light of another heaven, just as Dante emerged from the depths of hell, once again to see the stars.

I've heard tell of a poor harvest-hand who died in his hospital bed. When the priest had come to offer extreme unction and anoint his hands, he resisted opening his right hand in which he was clutching a few dirty coins—not perceiving that it would soon no more be his than he himself would be his. And so it is, we close up, not our hand but our heart, desiring to clutch within it the world.

If we die, die irrevocably, what is it all for? For what? It is the "why?" of the Sphinx. It is the "why?" that saps the marrow of the soul. It is the father of that anguish that breeds in us the love of hope.

Tragic the problem, ever present; the more we want to flee from it, the more we deliver ourselves to it. It was the serene Plato (serene?) who twenty-four centuries ago in his dialogue on the immortality of the soul, revealed his own doubt about our dream of being immortal, and the *risk* . . . !

Confronting the risk, I am presented with reasoning designed to do away with it, to prove the absurdity of the belief in the immortality of the soul. But this reasoning does not strike home with me. These are reasons, mere reasons, and it is not by such that the heart is set at peace. I do not want to die; I neither want it nor do I want to want it. I want to live on, on, on—to live, poor being that I am, as I know myself here, now, this "I"—and that is why the question of the duration of my soul, *my* soul, tortures me.

I am the center of my universe, the center of the universe. . . .

"And who are you?" you ask of me. . . . I reply: "For the universe, nothing; for me, everything!" Pride? Pride to want to be immortal? Poor humans! Tragic destiny, no doubt, to have to build one's belief in immortality upon such a slippery and shifting foundation stone as the desire for immortality.

I'm dreaming? Let me dream. For this dream is my life. Do not awaken me. I believe in the immortal origin of this yearning; it is the very essence of my soul. But . . . Do I really believe in it? "And why do you want to be immortal?" you ask me, Why? Frankly, I do not understand the question. You are asking about the reason for the reason, the purpose of the purpose, the motive for the motive.

But of such, matters there can be no speaking.

Section 2

Bertrand Russell

Chuang Tzu

Bertrand Russell

Bertrand Russell, 1872–1970, England. Russell was a major figure in the early twentieth century when analytical, logical, and mathematical methods replaced the metaphysical and speculative philosophies of the nineteenth century. His Principia Mathematica, *co-authored with Alfred North Whitehead, was a landmark work in modern philosophy. He later wrote on a variety of philosophical topics, with increasing emphasis on social and ethical issues.*

The selection that follows consists of an extract from his book, What I Believe.

It is only facts on or near the surface of the earth that we can, to some extent, mould to suit our desires. And even on the surface of the earth, our powers are very limited. Above all, we cannot prevent death, although we can often delay it.

Religion is an attempt to overcome this antithesis. If the world is controlled by God, and God can be moved by prayer, we acquire a share in omnipotence. In former days, miracles happened in answer to prayer; they still do in the Catholic Church, but Protestants have lost this power. However, it is possible dispense with miracles, since Providence has decreed that the operation of natural laws shall produce the best possible results. Thus belief in God still serves to humanize the world of nature, and to make men feel that physical forces are really their allies. In like manner immortality removes the terror from death. People who believe that when they die they will inherit eternal bliss may be expected to view death without horror, though, fortunately for medical men, this does not invariably happen. It does, however, soothe men's fears somewhat, even when it cannot allay them wholly.

Religion, since it has its source in terror, has dignified certain kinds of fear, and made people think them not disgraceful. In this it has done mankind a great disservice: *all* fear is bad, and ought to be overcome not by fairy tales, but by courage and rational reflection. I believe that when I die I shall rot, and nothing of my ego will survive. I am not young, and I love life. But I should scorn to shiver with terror at the thought of annihilation. Happiness is none the less true happiness because it must come to an end, nor do thought and love lose their value because they are not everlasting. Many a man has borne himself proudly on the scaffold: surely the same pride should teach us to think truly about man's place in the world.

Chuang Tzu

Chuang Tzu, circa fourth century B.C., *China. Chuang Chou (honorific name: Chuang Tzu) was one of the great philosophical figures of ancient China during the remarkable period of philosophical creativity circa 500* B.C. *to 200* B.C. *His writings, along with those attributed to Lao Tzu, are the great classics of the enormously influential philosophy of Taoism. Whereas the text of Lao Tzu consists of quasi-mystical, cryptic, and quasi-poetic stanzas, the text of Chuang Tzu is anecdotal, earthy, witty, and full of paradox.*

The translation and editing are mine.

What do I mean by a True Man? If he had little, or had no recognition, there was no complaining. If he came to high station, he didn't put on airs. So he could make a mistake and not be disturbed, and he could get things right without being self-satisfied. He could climb high without fear, enter the water without getting soaked. He could breach the fire but not be burned. He knew how to climb to the heights and follow the Way itself.

The True Man of ancient times slept a dreamless sleep. Awake, he had no cares, no hungers. His breath arose from deep down, from his very heels. But the common man's breath comes barely out his throat; it's as if he were vomiting out his words. His cravings are strong, so his commitment to the Way is weak.

The True Man of ancient times knew this: not to love life, not to hate death. He came into life without rejoicing, left it without resisting. He didn't forget where he'd come from, didn't worry about where he'd end. He enjoyed what he received, and handed it back without a thought. He came in briskly, left briskly—and that was that. . . .

Life and death are ordained by Heaven, just as the succession of night and day. That's the nature of things; we can't do anything about it.

The sage moves in a realm where things are stable and not constantly slipping away. So for him the end is as good as the beginning, and an early death is as good as reaching old age.

Master Yu became ill, and Ssu went to ask after him.

"It's remarkable!" said Yu. "The maker of things has made me so crooked that my back sticks way up, and my chin has sunk to my navel. My insides are upside down, my shoulders are above my head, and my neckbone is like a spine pointing up to the sky! The yin and the yang seem all out of kilter."

But Yu didn't fuss about it; he was inwardly at ease. He hobbled over to a well and gazed at his reflection. "Oh my! What a crumpled thing I've been made into!"

"Do you hate being in this condition?" asked Ssu.

"Why, no! Why should I? The way things go, my left arm may end up as a rooster and I'll be watching for the dawn. Or maybe my left arm will end up as a crossbow, and I'll bring down a good roasting bird. Or maybe after a time my rear end will have turned into a pair of cartwheels, and my spirit into a horse, and I'd go for a ride. I'd never need a carriage again!

"I get something because the time has come, and I lose it when the time comes. I take whatever time brings, I don't sorrow; I don't celebrate. In the old days this was called "getting free of the bonds." Some people can't manage to get free, and they remain in bondage. Such is our fate, and such it ever was. So why hate it?"

Shortly afterward, Lai grew ill. He lay gasping, at the point of death. Gathered round him, weeping and bemoaning his fate, were his wife and children. Li came to ask after him. "Shoo!" he said to the family. "Get back! Let the change take its course."

Then he leaned comfortably against the door and chatted with Lai. "Isn't it a wonderful process," Li said, "this change we go through? What do you think you'll turn into? A rat's liver? A bug's arm? Where will you be taken?"

Lai replied, "A child obeys his father and mother, and goes where he is told. The yin and yang are more to us than father or mother! They are taking me to my death. Should I rebel? Anyway it's pointless to defy them or to blame them. This great ball of mud gave shape to me, kept me toiling in order to keep alive, gave me ease in my old age, and now will give me rest in death. If I think life is good, then I have to think death is, too."

Yen Hui said to Confucius, "When Meng-sun Ts'ai's mother died, he wailed but he didn't shed any tears. He didn't really grieve. In fact he didn't even put on a show of sorrow in conducting the funeral. In spite of that he has a reputation everywhere in the country for handling funerals well. How does a man gain such a reputation with nothing solid to support it? To me it's a puzzle."

Confucius said, "Meng-sun did whatever needed doing. He wasn't negligent, though it might look as if he were. He has unusual wisdom. He doesn't claim to know why there is life, or why there is death. He doesn't know whether to press ahead or lag behind. The fact that all things continually change leaves him waiting for the next change but not pretending to know what it will bring. Besides, once he has changed, how would he know he has? And if it seems he hasn't yet changed, how would he know if that's so? Even if something startles his body, it won't disturb his spirit. Like an alarming noise in the house at night, when dawn comes there's nothing there. Meng-sun alone is awake. He did wail at the funeral—why?—simply because that's what's done at funerals.

You and I—maybe we're still asleep and dreaming. When I say "I," do I really know who "I" is? You dream you're a bird and fly high into the sky; you dream you're a fish diving down into a pool. You tell me about it, but how do I know whether we are dreaming or are awake?

There's no point in running to meet what comes. Better to just laugh, or even better than that, just go along. If you can be at ease about the changes, forget about them, then, though there's no map, you'll be on the right path.

Chuang Tzu was fishing in the P'u River when two officials came to him with this message from the king of Ch'u: "It is my desire that you should take up the weighty task of administering my realm."

Chuang Tzu didn't bother to turn his head, but just kept on fishing. He said, "I've heard there's a sacred tortoise in Ch'u, dead three thousand years. And I've heard the king keeps it wrapped in cloth in a case, and has it stored in the temple of his ancestors. Would that tortoise rather be dead and have its bones honored? Or would it rather be alive and dragging its tail in the mud?"

The officers replied: "It would rather be alive and dragging its tail in the mud."

Chuang Tzu said, "Go away! I'll drag my tail in the mud!"

Chuang Tzu's wife died, and Hui Tzu went to convey his condolences. Chuang Tzu was sitting, his legs sprawled out, pounding on a tub, and singing.

"You lived with her, she brought up your children, you grew old together," said Hui Tzu. "It's bad enough not to weep at her death. But pounding on a tub? That's too much!"

"Wrong," said Chuang Tzu. Do you think I didn't have any feelings when she died? But then I reflected, I went back to the very beginning, to the time before she was born, in fact to the time before she had a body, before she even had a spirit. In the Great Chaos there was a change, then another and another—and her spirit came into being. More change—and she had a body. Still more—she was born. So now there's been still another change—she's dead. It's like spring, summer, autumn, winter—change and transformation, the Way of things. Now she lies at peace in the Great Chamber. If I went on sobbing and wailing, it would mean I don't understand the Way and its transformations. But I stopped."

Lieh Tzu was traveling and stopped for a roadside meal. Under a bush he saw a hundred-year old skull. He turned to it and said: Only you and I know you aren't dead, and that you never lived. Are you satisfied? For that matter, am I?

Chuang Tzu was dying and his disciples wanted to give him a grand burial. But Chuang said that all the ceremonial needs were already there: "Heaven and earth will be my outer and inner coffin, the sun and moon my pair of jade discs, the stars in their constellations will be my pearl jewels, the myriad things of this world will be my mourners. Nothing is lacking. What could you add?"

"Master, we are afraid if we simply leave you the crows and kites will eat you."

"True, but below ground, I'll be eaten by the ants and worms. You want to take from one to give to the other. Why so?"

Section 3

Eugène Ionesco

Albert Camus

Eugène Ionesco

Eugène Ionesco, 1912–1994, France. Although born in Rumania, Ionesco spent most of his life in France and became one of France's leading playwrights. His plays, performed world-wide, are both witty and grim, and are generally considered to be central to the mid-twentieth-century "absurdist" theater.

The following selections are from Fragments of a Journal, *published in 1968.*

I could have done so many things, I could have realized so many dreams if weariness, an inconceivable, enormous weariness had not overpowered me for the last fifteen years or so, or even far longer. A weariness that kept me from working but also from resting, from enjoying life and being happy and relaxing, and that also kept me from turning more towards others, as I'd have wished to, instead of being the prisoner of myself, of my weariness, of that weight, that burden which is the burden of my self; how can you turn outwards towards others when your own self weighs you down? No doctor, and I've consulted thirty or forty of them, no doctor has known how to or been able to, cure this infinite weariness because, presumably, not one of them has gone to the source, the deep-seated cause of my trouble. I myself am increasingly aware of the reason for my exhaustion: it is that perennial doubt, the sense of 'What's the use?'

that seems to have been rooted in my mind all my life and that I cannot get rid of. Or, if that 'What's the use?' had not germinated in my soul, then shot up, then spread over everything, choking all other plants. . . .

I wonder how I can still be excited, or at any rate preoccupied, by economic, social and political problems since I know: (1) that we are going to die, (2) that revolution saves us neither from life nor from death, (3) that I cannot imagine a finite universe, an infinite universe, nor yet a universe that is neither finite nor infinite.

We are in life in order to die. Death is the aim of existence, that seems to be a commonplace truth. Sometimes, in a trite expression, the banality may vanish and truth appear, reappear, newborn. I am living through one of those moments when it seems to me that I am discovering for the first time that the only aim of existence is death. There's nothing we can do. There's nothing we can do. There's nothing we can do. But what sort of a puppet-like condition is this, what right have they to make a fool of me?

I still feel surprised, sometimes, that I'm no longer twelve years old.

On reading *Phaedo*, it's only towards the end of the dialogue that I realize what a fine mess we are in. Socrates has not managed to convince me that the soul is immortal and that he is going to live in a better world. You get the impression that Socrates' disciples are not convinced either, since they weep; otherwise, why should they weep? When evening comes and Socrates takes the poison, when his feet grow cold and then his stomach, when at last he dies, I am seized with terror and boundless unhappiness. The description of the death of Socrates is so convincing, far more convincing than his arguments for immortality. In any case, the arguments vanish in an instant; we forget them at once, but the image of Socrates dead is graven in my memory; all men are mortal, Socrates is a man, therefore

Socrates is mortal. I lay awake last night thinking about this. For a long time I had not felt such lucid, vivid, glacial anguish. A fear of nothingness.

It's impossible to understand anything about it. All those who fancy they do are fools. It's only when I say that everything is incomprehensible that I come as close as possible to understanding the only thing it is given to us to understand.

Nothing is mightier than our *why*, nothing stands above it, because in the end there is a *why* to which no answer is possible. In fact, from *why* to *why*, from one step to the next, you get to the end of things. And it is only by travelling from one *why* to the next, so far as the *why* that is unanswerable, that man attains the level of the creative principle, facing the infinite, equal to the infinite maybe. So long as he can answer the *why* he gets lost, he loses his way among things. 'Why this?' I answer, 'because that', and from one explanation to the next I reach the point where no explanation is satisfying, from one explanation to the next I reach zero, the absolute, where truth and falsehood are equivalent, become equal to one another, are identified with one another, cancel each other out in face of the absolute *nothing*. And so we can understand how all action, all choice, all history is justified, at the end of time, by a final cancelling-out. The *why* goes beyond everything. Nothing goes beyond the *why*, not even the *nothing*, because the *nothing* is not the explanation; when silence confronts us, the question to which there is no answer rings out in the silence. That ultimate *why*, that great *why* is like a light that blots out everything, but a blinding light; nothing more can be made out, there is nothing more to make out. . . .

It's to Death, above all, that I say 'Why'? with such terror. Death alone can, and will, close my mouth.

Here are some pages from a journal I kept five or six years ago, or some notes for *Exit the King,* which I was about to start writing. These fragments of dialogue were not inserted into the text of the play.

The Queen: How could you get so rooted in this world? you cling to it, you believe in the world, you dig your nails into these clouds, this unreal stuff which you take for reality, for rock. You see, it's giving way, it's breaking up, it's dissolving into clouds, flakes, snow, water, steam, smoke. You cling to it. . . . Try to loosen your hold, little by little. . . . Break the habit of living. How could you forget that all this is just a brief passage? you used to know that, you said you knew it. But you can't have known it. You were lying to yourself. You knew without really knowing.

The King: Let go, did you say? Nobody, nothing lets go willingly. A stone resists the pickaxe, wood resists when you split or break it; everything resists, fights back, defends itself, everything holds on and persists in holding on. A rat or an ant is terrified of death, fleas defend themselves, and microbes, everything that exists would rather kill than be killed. Everything clings to its own integrity. Everything seeks to devour the rest of the world, cankers spread, armies crush whole nations and put the conquered to the sword; they all want to take everything and give nothing . . . to destroy others and preserve themselves. Giving is the beginning of death. Oh, if only molecules could separate from one another of their own free will! It's the cohesion of my molecules that is responsible for my anguish. If only I could find out where the stitches are, take myself to pieces, undo the ligatures as one unties a knot of string! If I were unfastened, it would be easy. How can I untie this knot, how can I give up my will; or else will myself to be like water that can be poured into any vessel, thrown to the winds . . . or a vapour, or the wind; these are things that seem to suffer less than others when they disintegrate, there are no knots in them. But I am made up of tight knots, knots that resist, that insist on being knots. I cannot, I will not, I cannot, I will not.

Albert Camus

Albert Camus, 1913 - 1960, France. Camus was a leading writer and editor in the French Resistance in World War II. After the war, he became a preeminent novelist and essayist of international stature.

This selection is from the conclusion of his novel, The Stranger. *The protagonist, Meursault, has been sentenced to death; it is the eve of his execution.*

The chaplain looked at me with a kind of sadness. I now had my back flat against the wall, and light was streaming over my forehead. He muttered a few words I didn't catch and abruptly asked if he could embrace me. "No," I said. He turned and walked over to the wall and slowly ran his hand over it. "Do you really love this earth as much as all that?" he murmured. I didn't answer.

He stood there with his back to me for quite a long time. His presence was grating and oppressive. I was just about to tell him to go, to leave me alone, when all of a sudden, turning toward me, he burst out, "No, I refuse to believe you! I know that at one time or another you've wished for another life." I said of course I had, but it didn't mean any more than wishing to be rich, to be able to swim faster, or to have a more nicely shaped mouth. It was all the same. But he stopped me and

wanted to know how I pictured this other life. Then I shouted
at him, "One where I could remember this life!" and that's
when I told him I'd had enough. He wanted to talk to me
about God again, but I went up to him and made one last
attempt to explain to him that I had only a little time left and I
didn't want to waste it on God. He tried to change the subject
by asking me why I was calling him "monsieur" and not
"father." That got me mad, and I told him he wasn't my father;
he wasn't even on my side.

"Yes, my son," he said, putting his hand on my shoulder, "I
am on your side. But you have no way of knowing it, because
your heart is blind. I shall pray for you."

Then, I don't know why, but something inside me snapped. I
started yelling at the top of my lungs, and I insulted him and
told him not to waste his prayers on me. I grabbed him by the
collar of his cassock. I was pouring out on him everything that
was in my heart, cries of anger and cries of joy. He seemed so
certain about everything, didn't he? And yet none of his certain-
ties was worth one hair of a woman's head. He wasn't even sure
he was alive, because he was living like a dead man. Whereas it
looked as if I was the one who'd come up emptyhanded. But I
was sure about me, about everythihg, surer than he could ever
be, sure of my life and sure of the death I had waiting for me.
Yes, that was all I had. But at least I had as much of a hold on it
as it had on me. I had been right, I was still right, I was always
right. I had lived my life one way and I could just as well have
lived it another. I had done this and I hadn't done that. I hadn't
done this thing but I had done another. And so? It was as if I
had waited all this time for this moment and for the first light of
this dawn to be vindicated. Nothing, nothing mattered, and I
knew why. So did he. Throughout the whole absurd life I'd
lived, a dark wind had been rising toward me from somewhere
deep in my future, across years that were still to come, and as it
passed, this wind leveled whatever was offered to me at the time,
in years no more real than the ones I was living. What did other
people's deaths or a mother's love matter to me; what did his
God or the lives people choose or the fate they think they elect
matter to me when we're all elected by the same fate, me and

billions of privileged people like him who also called themselves my brothers? Couldn't he see, couldn't he see that? Everybody was privileged. There were only privileged people. The others would all be condemned one day. And he would be condemned, too. What would it matter if he were accused of murder and then executed because he didn't cry at his mother's funeral? . . . What did it matter that Raymond was as much my friend as Céleste, who was worth a lot more than him? What did it matter that Marie now offered her lips to a new Meursault? Couldn't he, couldn't this condemned man see. . . . And that from somewhere deep in my future. . . . All the shouting had me gasping for air. But they were already tearing the chaplain from my grip and the guards were threatening me. He calmed them, though, and looked at me for a moment without saying anything. His eyes were full of tears. Then he turned and disappeared.

With him gone, I was able to calm down again. I was exhausted and threw myself on my bunk. I must have fallen asleep, because I woke up with the stars in my face. Sounds of the countryside were drifting in. Smells of night, earth, and salt air were cooling my temples. The wondrous peace of that sleeping summer flowed throught me like a tide. Then, in the dark hour before dawn, sirens blasted. They were announcing departures for a world that now and forever meant nothing to me. For the first time in a long time I thought about Maman. I felt as if I understood why at the end of her life she had taken a "fiancé," why she had played at beginning again. Even there, in that home where lives were fading out, evening was a kind of wistful respite. So close to death, Maman must have felt free then and ready to live it all again. Nobody, nobody had the right to cry over her. And I felt ready to live it all again too. As if that blind rage had washed me clean, rid me of hope; for the first time, in that night alive with signs and stars, I opened myself to the gentle indifference of the world. Finding it so much like myself—so like a brother, really—I felt that I had been happy and that I was happy again. For everything to be consummated, for me to feel less alone, I had only to wish that there be a large crowd of spectators the day of my execution and that they greet me with cries of hate.

Section 4

Bhagavad Gita

Arthur Schopenhauer

Sigmund Freud

Bhagavad Gita

*The Bhagavad Gita (The Song of God), circa fourth century
B.C., India. This is one of the central texts of Hinduism, and has
been widely influential in the West as a text representing Asian
thought. It is a more or less autonomous segment of a very long
epic poem, the* Mahabharata.

*The setting of the Bhagavad Gita is that of two great armies
confronting each other and about to go into battle. However, the
armies represent different branches of the same family, and thus
the battle will be a fratricidal one. Arjuna is a heroic figure and
a leader of one of the armies. His ally and charioteer is Krishna,
who is in fact an incarnation of the great God Vishnu. As the two
are about to go into battle, Arjuna holds back, to Krishna's surprise, and puts his dilemma to Krishna. The translation and editing are mine.*

Arjuna spoke:

Lord, how can I send arrows in battle against my venerable
teachers and kinsmen? Even if they are moved by hope of gain,
it would be better for me to live by begging than to enjoy a life
stained with their blood.

Which would be better?—That we should conquer them, or
they us? We do not know. If we were to slay them, we ourselves
would no longer wish to live.

I am overcome by despair, confused as to my duty. I am your pupil, Lord, a suppliant asking for guidance. I cannot see how even the greatest kingdom on earth, or even godly power, could dispel my grief.

Lord, I will not fight.

With a gentle smile, the Lord Krishna replied to Arjuna in his desperation as he stood there between the armies that faced each other:

Arjuna, you mourn for those who are not to be mourned. You only talk the language of wisdom; those who are truly wise mourn neither the living or the dead. There was never a time when you, or I, or those noble kinsmen did not exist, nor will there ever hereafter be a time when any of us will not exist.

That spirit which lives in this body goes with it from childhood to youth to old age, then it departs this body and goes on to live in a new body. There is nothing perplexing in this for those who are truly wise. Just as one discards worn-out clothes, so we discard the worn-out body and take on a new one.

It is bodily sensations—cold, heat, pleasure, pain—that come and go. They are transitory. Endure them, but do not be disturbed by them. For the truly wise, pleasure and pain are in this alike. The wise transcend mortality.

Nothing can come into being from nonbeing. Nor can being become nonbeing. Those who have true knowledge understand this. The universe is what-is, and so no one can make it not be. And the Being that lives in the body is indestructible, even though the body as such is perishable.

Therefore, Arjuna, go into battle and fight! Whoever thinks of someone as a slayer, or as slain, fails to understand that what lives within can neither slay nor be slain. For what lives within the body is itself never born, never dies. Having being, it will always be. This inner being is primeval, eternal. It is not slain when the body is slain. Knowing this, what sense can it make to think you slay, or can cause anyone else to slay?

What lives within cannot be cut by weapons, burned by fire, dampened by water or dried by wind. It is ever the same, and so there is nothing to grieve about.

Indeed, Arjuna, even if you think of what lives within as continually being born and dying, there is no reason to be sorrowful. If born, death is certain; and for the dead, rebirth is certain. Understanding that this is inevitable, one has no reason to grieve, no reason to lament.

Do that which is thy duty. Act—but without attachment. . . . In that way one attains the highest. Act with the body alone, without personal desire, with self-restraint and a controlled mind. In that way there is no guilt. When personal desires and aims are kept out of all your undertakings, you will deserve to be called wise, and the fire of knowledge will consume your karma.

Arthur Schopenhauer

Arthur Schopenhauer, 1788–1860, Germany. Schopenhauer was a philosopher influenced by the tradition of German philosophy, especially Kant, and also by the philosophies of Hinduism. His outlook on human existence was dark, and he portrayed the will as a metaphysical force that drives human beings and generates pain, a force that must be subdued if spiritual liberation is to be achieved. He wrote technical philosophical works and also many informal essays on the human condition.

The selection that follows is from his major work, The World as Will and Idea. *The translation is mine.*

It cannot be denied that, at least in Europe, opinion frequently wavers—indeed often in the very same individual—between a view of death as absolute annihilation, and the assumption that, skin and bones, we are immortal. Both views are equally false. . . .

. . . the fear of death is independent of Reason. Animals have the fear; yet they do not know death. Every creature born into the world brings this fear with it. This a priori fear of death is simply the other face of the Will to Live, which is what we all are. Just as the concern for self-preservation is innate, so too, therefore, is the fear of one's own destruction. It is this, not the avoidance of pain, which is manifested by the anxious carefulness with which creatures seek to protect themselves and their brood from anything that can pose a danger. Why do creatures tremble and flee, trying to conceal themselves? It is the pure Will to Live. . . .

That powerful; clinging to life is blind and irrational, explicable only by the fact that we are in our whole nature the Will to Live. That is why it is our nature to value life as the highest good, no matter how embittered, short, and uncertain it ever is; for in its original nature Will is blind, unknowing.

Were it the thought of our nonbeing that made death seem so frightening, we ought to shudder, too, at the thought of the time before we ever came to be. For it is incontrovertible that the condition of nonbeing after death is no different from that before birth. Therefore the one can be no more lamentable than the other. We do not grieve at all that an eternity has gone by during which we did not yet exist. After this momentary and ephemeral interlude, an eternity will again go by; but this we find hard, indeed unbearable.

Now let us change our standpoint from that of death as viewed by the individual. In contrast, we will examine death from the standpoint of Nature as a whole. In so doing, however, our study will remain empirically grounded.

Admittedly, we know no greater game of chance than the game of life and death. Here every decision is faced with supreme suspense, concern, fear. In our eyes, it is all or nothing. On the other hand Nature, ever honest and open, does not lie. It speaks very differently on the theme, much as Krishna does in the Bhagavad Gita. Its testimony is that nothing at all rides on the life or death of the individual. It evidences this by abandoning both animal and human life to utterly meaningless accident, with no move toward rescue.

If we contemplate the world of insects in autumn, we see how one prepares its bed for sleep during the long, numbing winter-sleep, how another spins its cocoon in order to pass the Winter as chrysalis, awakening rejuvenated and perfected with the coming of Spring. In the end, most take thought for their peaceful rest in the arms of Death. They carefully arrange a suitable place into which to fit their eggs, in order to come forth, renewed. This is Nature's great teaching of immortality, which should bring us to the realization that there is no radical difference between sleep and death. . . .

. . . and so it is with you, deluded questioner; in this misunderstanding of your own nature you are no different from the leaves on the tree. In autumn they wilt and fall, and wail over their doom. They will not take comfort in the prospect of the fresh greening that will bedeck the tree in Spring. Instead they complain, "That is not I—it is quite another leaf." O foolish leaf!

So it is, everything lingers for a moment and hurries on toward death.

. . . it is the species that ever lives. When conscious of its identity with the everlasting species, the individual is of good cheer.

Could one bring this unity of being clearly into consciousness, there would be no difference between the continuing existence of the external world after one's death, and one's own continued existence after death.

As a mental experiment, make the effort to imagine vividly the time—not so distant after all—when you will have died. You think of yourself as absent; you let the world continue. Very soon, however, you discover to your surprise that you are still present. You meant to imagine the world without you, but consciousness and the "I" are inseparable. The "I" is that through which the world is first mediated, and to which alone it is present. The "I" is the center of all being, the nucleus of all reality. The experiment requires that you annul it, yet let the world continue. This is something that can be stated in the abstract, but not concretely thought.

. . . the feeling forces itself upon us that the world is no less in us than we are in it, and that the source of all reality lies within us. The result is actually this: Objectively the time when I will not be will come, but subjectively it can never come. . . .

At the beginning of this chapter I discussed the fact that this powerful clinging to life—or perhaps better said, fearing of death—in no way arises out of Reason, for then the result would be that the value of life would be known. Rather, all fear of death is directly rooted in the Will.

While individual consciousness does not survive death, what does survive is that which struggles against death: the Will. . . . So the fear of death remains, immutable, because it resides not in Reason but in the Will.

Actually, egoism resides in the fact that, for us, all reality is bounded by our own person; it exists as a perception in us, not in others. Death teaches better: The individual is in death made nul, but our essence, which is our Will, lives thereafter in others.

A truly good human being finds death's rule quiet and easy. But to die willingly, to die gladly, joyfully—that is the privilege of the resigned, of those who surrender, who say No to the Will to Live. Only that person genuinely, and not merely seemingly, wills to die. Only that person neither needs nor desires personal preservation.

Sigmund Freud

*Sigmund Freud, 1856–1939, Austria. Freud was the origina-
tor of psychoanalytic theory and practice, and was the recognized
leader of the movement until his death. The influence of psychoanalysis, both direct and indirect, was world wide.*

*The following consists of extracts from two of Freud's essays
written during World War I. The first selection comes from a portion of his 1915 essay, Thoughts for the "Times on War and
Death." The second selection is from his 1915 essay, "The Transitory." The translations are mine.*

I

One thing that leads me to infer that we feel so estranged in
this once so lovely world, where we felt so at home, is the dis-
turbance in our formerly well established attitude towards
death.

Our attitude was not sincere. Were one to hear us, we were
of course quite ready to acknowledge that all life necessarily
ends in death, that each one of us owes nature a death and must
be prepared to pay the debt—in short, that death is natural,
undeniable and unavoidable. In reality we were all careful to
behave as if it were otherwise. We demonstrated an unmistak-
able tendency to cast death aside, to eliminate it from life. We

sought to kill it with silence. We have the saying: "To think of something as if thinking of death"—one's own, of course.

Indeed one's own death is unimaginable. In any attempt to imagine it we can observe that we actually remain present as an observer. So it was that psychoanalysis could venture this proposition: At bottom, no one believes in his own death. Or, what comes to the same, In the Unconscious, each of us is convinced of his immortality.

Where the death of someone else is concerned, the person of culture will carefully avoid speaking of it in the hearing of that person. Only children pay no attention to such restraints; they threaten each other fearlessly with the prospect of death. They are even able to say, right to the face of one they love, such a thing as, "Dear Mama, it would be sad if you had died, but I'm going to do this or that. . . ."

The cultivated adult will not be inclined even to think about the death of someone else without seeming hardhearted or mean to himself—that is, unless he be under a professional duty, as physician, attorney, or such, to deal with death. Least of all will he permit himself to think of the death of someone else if that event is linked to bringing him freedom, or possessions.

Naturally our delicate feelings do not prevent the actual occurrence of death; when this takes place we are always deeply moved and as if shaken by the unexpected. We regularly emphasize the adventitious character of the cause of death—accident, illness, infection, advanced age—and in this we betray our effort to downgrade death from a necessity to a fortuitous happening. Where the event entails multiple deaths, this is something absolutely horrible to us.

Toward those who have died we show a special restraint, almost admiration for one who has managed so difficult a task. We cease criticism of such persons, we overlook their possible misdeeds, and pronounce the commandment: *De mortuis nil nisi bene*. We find it justified that in the funeral oration and on the gravestone it is the person's major virtues that are told. Consideration for the dead—which they no longer need—is more important to us than the truth, and certainly for most of us it's more important than consideration for the living.

This conventional-cultural attitude toward death is complemented by our complete breakdown if anyone near and dear to us—a parent, a brother or sister, a child, or other family member, or a dear friend—has met with death. With them we bury our hopes, our ambitions, our pleasures. We will not let ourselves be consoled, they shall not be replaced. We behave as if we were an Arabian Asra in Heine's poem, who "also die when those they love meet death."

However this way of relating to death has a great effect on our life. Life is impoverished; it loses interest when the highest stake in the game of life—life itself—must not be wagered. It becomes pallid, as shallow as a kind of American flirtation, in which it is understood at the outset that nothing will come of it, in contrast to a Continental love affair, in which each partner must ever have in mind the seriousness of the consequences. Our emotional ties, the unbearable intensity of our grief, make us averse to risk danger for ourselves or for our loved ones. We dare not even consider a number of projects which, though dangerous, are truly imperative projects, such as experiments in flight, expeditions to distant lands, experiments with explosive substances. We are paralyzed by the worry as to who shall replace the son for the mother, the wife for the husband, the father for the children, if misfortune strikes. The inclination to exclude death from our calculations about life brings as a consequence so many other renunciations and exclusions. Hence the motto of the Hanseatic League proclaims: *Navigare necesse est, vivere non necesse!* To sail the sea is necessary; to live is not.

How could it be otherwise, then, that we should seek in literature and in theater a substitute for what we have lost in life? There we find people who know how to die, and even how to bring others to their death. There alone can we manage what is required for us to reconcile ourselves to death, for through all the vicissitudes of life there is still something that remains immune. So it is sad indeed that it is in life as it is in chess, where a false move can force us to give up the game, with the difference that we have no second chance at a return game. In the world of fiction we find the many lives we need. Identifying ourselves with the hero, we die—outliving him forever, prepared to die a second time, unharmed, with another hero.

It is obvious that the War is sure to sweep away this conventional approach to death. Death will no longer be denied; it demands belief. People really do die, not only one by one but in numbers, often ten thousand a day. And no longer is it an accident. True, it is accidental whether this bullet hits this one rather than that one, but a second bullet may easily hit that one, too. The mass effect puts an end to the idea of accident. Indeed, life has once again become interesting; it has retrieved its full meaning.

We ask: What is the attitude of our Unconscious toward the problem of death? The answer rings out: Almost exactly the same as that of primeval man. In this, as in so many other respects, primitive man continues to live unchanged in our Unconscious. Indeed our Unconscious does not believe in our own death; it conducts itself as if immortal. What we call our "Unconscious" lies at the deepest instinct-driven strata of the mind. It knows nothing negative, no negation. Contradictories dwell side by side in it. Hence it does not know its own death, to which only negative content can be ascribed.

Nothing in the instinctual drives can lead us to the belief in death. This, perhaps, is the secret of heroism. The rational basis for heroism is the judgment that one's own life cannot be of as much value as certain abstract and general values. But to my mind, more frequent is that instinctual and impulsive heroism which takes no account of such motives, and in spite of the danger, relies simply on the confidence of Anzengruber's Blockhead-Hans—"Can't nothin' happen to ya." Or reasoning merely clears the way in one's mind for the heroic response that actually arises out of the Unconscious, a response that might otherwise be restrained. On the other hand, the fear of death, which reigns within us more often than we know, is something secondary and the result of guilt feelings.

However we do acknowledge death for strangers and enemies, and we award it to them just as willingly and unconcernedly as did primeval man. Here a distinction presents itself, one that in the real world is held to be decisive. Our Unconscious does not carry out the killing, it merely thinks it and wishes it. Still, it would be wrong to wholly devalue the significance of the similarity that does exist between *psychic* reality and *factual* reality. It is quite significant and consequential. Daily, hourly, we cast out from the realm of our Unconscious drives all who have stood in our way, all who have caused us insult or injury. "The Devil take you!"—that phrase which so often comes to our lips in angry jest, really says, "Death take you." In our Unconscious it is a serious, intense death-wish. Yes, our Unconscious murders even for trivial reasons, just as the ancient Athenian Draconic Code knew no other punishment for crime than death. This has the particular consequence that any damage to our almighty and all-sufficient Ego amounts to *lèse majesté*.

For the most part, psychoanalysis finds little credence among the lay public for propositions such as these. They are rejected as calumnies which Consciousness assures us are out of the question. Those faint clues through which the Unconscious betrays them to Consciousness are adeptly overlooked.

There is one case in which, for us just as for primeval man, there emerge together and in conflict the two contradictory attitudes to death: The recognition that death is the annihilation of life, and the rejection of this as unreal. This is the case where, as in primeval time, death or the threat of death was faced by our loved ones, parents, brothers, sisters, children, or dear friends. These loved ones are on one hand our inward possessions, constituents of our own Ego, and yet on the other hand, they are in part alien to us, even enemies. With few exceptions, the tenderest and most intimate of our love relationships contain a bit of enmity which can evoke the unconscious death-wish. However this ambivalence no longer gives rise to religious and ethical teachings but to neurosis, which in turn allows deep insights into normal mental life.

Let us sum up: Our Unconscious is quite impervious to the idea of our own death, murderous toward strangers, and, just as in primeval times, ambivalent toward loved ones.

Yet in our conventional-cultural attitude to death how far we have come from the original primeval state!

II

Some while ago I strolled through a flowering summer countryside in company with a friend of a contemplative nature, and with a young but already well known poet. The poet admired the beauty of Nature around us, but could take no pleasure in it. He was disturbed by the thought that all this beauty was destined to pass away, that come Winter it would have faded away—as it is with all human beauty, too, with everything beautiful and noble that humankind has created or could create. Everything that he would otherwise have loved and admired seemed to him to lose all value because it was destined to be transitory.

We know that this vulnerability of all that is beautiful or perfect is a fact that can evoke two different mental impulses. One leads to the painful worldweariness of the young poet, the other to rebellion against the fact as asserted. That all the magnificence of Nature and of Art, of the world of our feelings and the

world external to us—that all should pass away into Nothingness—No, it is impossible. To believe it would be too nonsensi-
cal, sinful. It must be possible that in some form or other all
this can continue to exist, and all destructive influences kept at
bay.

This demand for immortality cannot be put forward as a
realistic claim, however. It too obviously results from what we
wish were so. And yet, even what is painful can be true. I could
not bring myself to challenge the reality of this all-encompass-
ing transcience, nor could I argue that at least the beautiful and
the perfect are exceptions. But I did challenge the pessimistic
poet's claim that the transitoriness of the beautiful entails its
loss of value.

On the contrary—An increase in value! The value of transitoriness is a scarcity value within Time. Limits on the opportunity for pleasure heighten its preciousness. I declared it to be
incomprehensible that the thought of the transitory nature of
the beautiful could spoil our joy in it. So far as Nature's beauty
is concerned, it returns after Winter's destruction when the new
year comes. This recurrence may be taken as the form of the
eternal so far as the continuation of our existence goes. In our
own lives, the beauty of the human body and visage inevitably
disappear, but this brevity of existence lends added charm. A
flower may bloom only a single night; we see it as no less splen-
did. Nor can I see in the least how the beauty and perfection of
a work of art or an intellectual achievement should lose their
value because of their temporal limits.

A time may come when the pictures and statues that today
we so admire will decay, or when a race comes after us that can
no longer understand our poets and thinkers, or even when
there comes a geological epoch in which all life on earth has
been reduced to silence. The value of all this beauty and perfection will be determined only by the meaning it has had for our
own sensibility. This needs no survival, and therefore it is independent of absolute duration.

I took these considerations to be unarguable. I did note,
however, that I had made no impression on either the poet or

on my friend. From this failure I inferred that a strong emotional factor interfered, and that it clouded their judgment. Later, I believed I had found out what this was. It must have been the mind's rebellion against mourning, which for them entailed that the value of pleasure in the beautiful had also died. The idea that the beautiful is transitory produced in the feelings of both men a foretaste of mourning over its loss, and since the mind instinctively shrinks from pain, they felt their pleasure in the beautiful had been diminished, blighted by the thought of its transitoriness.

Section 5

Marcus Aurelius

Michel de Montaigne

David Hume

Marcus Aurelius

Marcus Aurelius, 121 A.D.–180 A.D., Rome. Marcus Aurelius was of that rare species, an emperor who was also a philosopher. Although Marcus Aurelius, as Roman emperor, was continuously occupied with the repression of rebellions and the campaign against the widely acknowledged threat of Christianity, he was at the same time a philosophically reflective writer. His Meditations *have remained a classic exposition of the then highly influential Stoic philosophy.*

The following is a modern translation by Colin F. Hasse, and consists of extracts from the Meditations.

Since you might depart this life at any time, govern your actions, words, and thoughts accordingly. Leaving the world of mankind is nothing to be afraid of, if the gods do exist, for they will do you no harm. If on the other hand they do not exist, or do not care about what happens in human affairs, why go on living in a universe without either gods or goodness? But they do exist, and they do care,

If you look carefully at dying for what it is in itself, and with the analysis of your reason you strip away all the images you

associate with death, you will find it to be an entirely natural process. And anyone who fears a natural process is a mere child.

The longest-lived and shortest-lived of men lose equally when they die. All any man has to lose is only his present, since he cannot in fact lose what he does not own—neither his past nor what he anticipates for his future.

You embarked, you made the voyage, you have arrived at the far shore. Now step ashore. If you land in a new life, there will be gods enough for you . . . if you step into nothing, a condition without consciousness, you will still be free of the constraints of your earthly body, of pain and pleasure.

Death is like birth, another of nature's secrets, a synthesis formed of identical elements and a dissolution back into them again. This is not a thing for which a man should be ashamed, since it is in no way contrary to his natural state as a rational being.

Always recall how many physicians are now dead, after much knitting of brows over their patients; how many astrologers dead, after much portentous foretelling of other men's deaths as though they were consequential events; how many philosophers dead after endless debate on death and immortality; how many famed warriors dead, after killing such multitudes; how many tyrants dead after exercising their powers of life and death with monumental arrogance, as though themselves immortal;

and how many cities are—if I may use the term so—also dead:
Helike, Pompeii, Herculaneum, innumerable others.

Remember also all those you have known, one after another.
One man closed a friend's eyes in death, and was then himself
laid out on his bier. Then the friend who closed his eyes was
buried by another—all of this within a short span of time. This
is the whole of it; never overlook how ephemeral and worthless
human things are. What was yesterday life-semen tomorrow will
be mummy, or ashes. Therefore, journey through this small
span of time in accord with nature, and come to your journey's
end content, just as an olive falls, when ripe: praising earth
which bore it and grateful to the tree on which it grew.

A commonplace yet still useful aid in facing death unafraid is
to reflect on those we know who have clung long and tena-
ciously to life. How are they better off than those who died pre-
maturely? All of them lie in their graves at last . . . even though
they buried many during their long lives, they were finally
buried themselves. On the whole, the difference between a long
life and a short one is insignificant, especially considering how
many tribulations there are, what sort of companions, and in
how weak a body this life is laboriously lived. Do not, therefore,
consider life a thing of much value. Look instead at the immen-
sity of time already past, and the infinity still ahead. In this eternity, a baby born but three days ago and a Nestor who has lived
past three generations are as one.

Make no distinction in doing your duty whether you are
cold or warm, drowsy or sated with sleep, whether defamed or

praised, or whether you are in process of dying, or of doing any other business. For the act of dying too is one of the acts of life, and it is sufficient even then to 'make the best use of the moment.'

To fear death is to fear either losing all sensation or finding a new, unfamiliar sensation. But if you no longer have any sensation, you will have no sensation of any evil either; likewise, if you should find new sensations, you will be a different kind of living being, but a living creature still.

Do not disdain death, but be content to accept it, since it too is one of the processes which nature ordains. For dissolution of life is part of nature, just as it is part of nature to be young and to be old; to grow up and to grow old; to grow first teeth, then beard, then grey hairs; to beget, to be pregnant, and to give birth; and to move through the rest of the natural functions which the seasons of your life bring. A reasoning man, therefore, will not be careless nor over-eager nor disdainful towards death, but will await it as one of nature's inevitable processes.

As you perform each act in your life, pause and ask yourself this: Is death to be dreaded because it would deprive you of this deed, this act?

No man is so fortunate that someone will not be at his deathbed welcoming the end which is befalling him. Even supposing that he is a serious and wise man, someone will be there at the last to say: "We can breathe freely again, now we are relieved of this disciplinarian! I can't actually say that he was hard on any one of us, but I knew that he was condemning us in his heart." So much for the serious and wise man. In the case of each of us, however, how numerous the reasons for so many to want to be quit of us! If you consider this when you are dying, you will depart the more easily.

Consider that in a little while you will be no one and nowhere, nor will anything you now see nor anyone who now lives still exist.

Michel de Montaigne

Michel de Montaigne, 1533–1592, France. Montaigne was one of the earliest and greatest of European essayists. His Essays *have become a classic exemplar of humanism. The impact of his work has come not only from the content of these essays but also by reason of the style, whose vigor and color have made his outlook and his personality a living influence through the centuries.*

The selection that follows is chapter 20 of his Essays, *and is entitled: "To Philosophise is to Learn to Die." The translation is mine.*

Cicero said that philosophizing is naught but preparing for death.

. . . as for death, it is inevitable. . . . and if in consequence it makes us fear, it is a continual torment that can in no way be alleviated. There is nowhere that it does not arise, turn as we may, this way or that.

At the end of the race is death; of necessity we aim at it. If it frightens us, how can we possibly move ahead without trembling?

The common remedy is not to think about it. People are frightened if one even mentions death. Most cross themselves as if the devil had been invoked. And because it is mentioned in one's will, you can't even expect people to turn to the matter until a physician has pronounced their doom. Then, between pain and fear, their judgments in the matter are God knows what.

How many ways death has to surprise! . . . Who would ever have thought that a Duke of Brittany would be smothered by the crowd, as happened to him on the entrance into the city of Pope Clement . . .? And didn't you see one of our kings killed on the jousting field? And one of his ancestors dying after being knocked down by a hog?

. . . how is it possible for a man to put aside the thought of death, how can it fail to seem to us at each instant that death has us by the throat? "What does it matter;" you'll say to me, "however things may be, provided one pays no attention to it?" I'm of that opinion, too, and in whatever way one can shield oneself from the blows, even if it were to hide under a calfskin, I'm not the man to draw back from it. For me it is enough if I can spend my time at my ease, and take what recreation I best can. . . .

They come, they go, they run, they dance—but nothing said of death. That's lovely. But when it does arrive, either to themselves, their wives, children, or friends, taking them by surprise, what torments, what wailing, what frenzy, and what despair overcome them! Did you ever see such downheartedness, such ado, such turmoil? One should prepare for it at an earlier time.

Let us learn to stand firm and fight it. And let us begin by denying death its greatest advantage—let us follow a path contrary to what is common. Let us strip away its strangeness, engage with it, accustom ourselves to it, having nothing more frequently in mind than death. At every instant let us have it before our imagination, in all its guises. At the stumbling of a horse, the fall of a stone, the slightest prick of a pin, let us think to ourself: Well, and what if *this* were finally death? And thereupon let us be strong of heart, strong of will. Amidst feasts and pleasures we should always keep in mind the remembrance of our condition, never let ourselves be so carried away with pleasures that our memory fails to remind us how many are the ways that our happiness can fall prey to death, how many are the ways she threatens us. . . .

Forethought of death is forethought of freedom. Who has learned to die, has unlearned servility. Knowing how to die frees one from all subjection, all constraints.

There is nothing that I have ever occupied myself with more than my imaginings of death—even in the most licentious period of my life.

One should always be ready booted to depart, insofar as in us is possible, taking care that there is no business undone except what pertains to oneself. . . . I am in such a condition now, I thank God, that I can leave here when it pleases Him, regretting nothing, except only life itself if its loss should weigh on me. I have undone all ties; my adieus to everyone except myself are half given. Never has any man prepared himself to leave the world more purely, more fully, and totally than I expect to do. A man should not have large undertakings; or at least not have a passionate commitment to seeing them to the end. But we are born to act. . . . My wish is that people should act, act so as to prolong the doings of life as much as possible, and for Death to find me planting my cabbages, without care that he comes, even less that my garden work is unfinished.

Our religion has no more solid human foundation than the contempt for life. . . . What does it matter when death comes if it is inevitable? To one who said to Socrates, "The thirty tyrants have condemned you to death," Socrates replied, "And Nature them."

As our birth brought the birth of all things, so our death brings the death of all things. The folly of weeping because we will not be alive a hundred years hence is just the same as that of weeping because we were not alive a hundred years ago. Out of death comes another life.

Nothing can warrant grief if it be but once. Is it reasonable to fear for so long a thing that is so brief? Long life, or short life—death makes them one.

Life of itself is neither good nor bad—it is the place in which the good and the bad exist, accordingly as you bring them about.

How simpleminded to condemn what you have never experienced, either in yourself or anyone else!

David Hume

David Hume, 1711–1776, Scotland. Hume was one of the towering figures in the history of Western philosophy. He wrote major works on English history and political issues, but his philosophical writings on theory of knowledge and ethics remain landmarks that today are still the subject of active study and discussion among philosophers.

The first selection that follows consists of extracts from Hume's essay, "On Suicide." The second selection is from a letter written by Adam Smith, the great economic theorist and good friend of Hume's, and addressed to William Strahan, a mutual acquaintance. In the letter Smith describes how Hume, mortally ill from a lingering illness, confronted death.

I

So great is our horror of death, that when it presents itself, under any form, besides that to which a man has endeavored to reconcile his imagination, it acquires new terrors and overcomes his feeble courage: But when the menaces of superstition are joined to this natural timidity, no wonder it quite deprives men of all power over their life, since even many pleasures and enjoyments, to which we are carried by a strong propensity, are torn from us by this inhuman tyrant. Let us here endeavour to restore men to their native liberty by examining all the common arguments against Suicide, and shewing that that action may be free from every imputation of guilt or blame, according to the sentiments of all the ancient philosophers.

If Suicide be criminal, it must be a transgression of our duty either to God, our neighbour, or ourselves—To prove that suicide is no transgression of our duty to God, the following considerations may perhaps suffice. In order to govern the material world, the almighty Creator has established general and immutable laws by which all bodies, from the greatest planet to the smallest particle of matter, are maintained in their proper sphere and function. . . .

What is the meaning then of that principle, that a man who, tired of life, and hunted by pain and misery, bravely overcomes all the natural terrors of death and makes his escape from this cruel scene; that such a man, I say, has incurred the indignation of his Creator by encroaching on the office of divine providence, and disturbing the order of the universe? Shall we assert that the Almighty has reserved to himself in any peculiar manner the disposal of the lives of men, and has not submitted that event, in common with others, to the general laws by which the universe is governed? This is plainly false; the lives of men depend up the same laws as the lives of all other animals; and these are subjected to the general laws of matter and motion. . . .

. . . it is no encroachment on the office of providence to disturb or alter these general laws: Has not every one, of consequence, the free disposal of his own life? And may he not lawfully employ that power with which nature has endowed him? In order to destroy the evidence of this conclusion, we must shew a reason, why this particular case is excepted; is it because human life is of so great importance, that "tis a presumption for human prudence to dispose of it? But the life of a man is of no greater importance to the universe than that of an oyster. . . .

Do you imagine that I repine at providence or curse my creation, because I go out of life, and put a period to a being, which, were it to continue, would render me miserable? Far be such sentiments from me; I am only convinced of a matter of fact, which you yourself acknowledge possible, that human life may be unhappy, and that my existence, if further prolonged, would become ineligible: but I thank providence, both for the good which I have already enjoyed, and for the power with which I am endowed of escaping the ill that threatens me. To you it belongs to repine at providence, who foolishly imagine that you have no such power, and who must still prolong a hated life, tho' loaded with pain and sickness, with shame and poverty.—Do you not teach, that when any ill befalls me, tho' by the malice of my enemies, I ought to be resigned to providence, and that the actions of men are the operations of the Almighty as much as the actions of inanimate beings? When I fall upon my own sword, therefore, I receive my death equally from the hands of the Deity as if it had proceeded from a lion, a precipice, or a fever. . . .

There is no being, which possesses any power or faculty, that it receives not from its Creator, nor is there any one, which by ever so irregular an action can encroach upon the plan of his providence, or disorder the universe. . . .

When the horror of pain prevails over the love of life; when a voluntary action anticipates the effects of blind causes; 'tis only in consequence of those powers and principles, which he has implanted in his creatures. . . .

A man, who retires from life, does no harm to society: He only ceases to do good; which, if it is an injury, is of the lowest kind.—All our obligations to do good to society seem to imply something reciprocal. I receive the benefits of society and therefore ought to promote its interests, but when I withdraw myself altogether from society, can I be bound any longer? But, allowing that our obligations to do good were perpetual, they have certainly some bounds; I am not obliged to do a small good to society at the expence of a great harm to myself why then should I prolong a miserable existence, because of some frivolous advantage which the public may perhaps receive from me? If upon account of age and infirmities I may lawfully resign any office, and employ my time altogether in fencing against these calamities, and alleviating as much as possible the miseries of my future life: Why may I not cut short these miseries at once by an action which is no more prejudicial to society? . . . .

For such is our natural horror of death, that small motives will never be able to reconcile us to it; and though perhaps the situation of a man's health or fortune did not seem to require this remedy, we may at least be assured, that any one who, without apparent reason, has had recourse to it, was curst with such an incurable depravity or gloominess of temper as must poison all enjoyment, and render him equally miserable as if he had been loaded with the most grievous misfortunes.—If suicide be supposed a crime, 'tis only cowardice can impel us to it. If it be no crime, both prudence and courage should engage us to rid ourselves at once of existence, when it becomes a burthen.

II

[While mortally ill, Hume was reading Lucian's Dialogue of the Dead, and said that] among all the excuses which are alleged to

Charon for not entering readily into his boat, he could not find one that fitted him; he had no house to finish, he had no daughter to provide for, he had no enemies upon whom he wished to revenge himself. 'I could not well imagine,' said he, 'what excuse I could make to Charon in order to obtain a little delay. I have done every thing of consequence which I ever meant to do, and I could at no time expect to leave my relations and friends in a better situation than that in which I am now likely to leave them; I, therefore, have all reason to die contented.' He then diverted himself with inventing several jocular excuses, which he supposed he might make to Charon, and with imagining the very surly answers which it might suit the character of Charon to return to them. 'Upon further consideration,' said he, 'I thought I might say to him, Good Charon, I have been correcting my works for a new edition. Allow me a little time, that I may see how the Public receives the alterations.' But Charon would answer, 'When you have seen the effect of these, you will be for making other alterations. There will be no end of such excuses; so, honest friend, please step into the boat.' But I might still urge, 'Have a little patience, Good Charon, I have been endeavouring to open the eyes of the Public. If I live a few years longer, I may have the satisfaction of seeing the downfall of some of the prevailing systems of superstition.' But Charon would then lose all temper and decency. 'You loitering rogue, that will not happen these many hundred years. Do you fancy I will grant you a lease for so long a term? Get into the boat this instant, you lazy loitering rogue.'

[Hume] continued to the last perfectly sensible, and free from much pain or feelings of distress. He never dropped the smallest expression of impatience; but when he had occasion to speak to the people about him, always did it with affection and tenderness. . . . When he became very weak, it cost him an effort to speak, and he died in such a happy composure of mind, that nothing could exceed it.

INDEX